The Saudi-Egyptian Conflict over North Yemen, 1962–1970

About the Book and Author

The 1962 coup d'état in North Yemen initiated one of the most debilitating Middle East conflicts ever, the eight-year civil war in North Yemen. This conflict in an obscure corner of the Arab world eventually assumed global importance, attracting the attention of the superpowers and the United Nations.

This book focuses on the Yemeni civil war's impact at the regional level, where it provoked enmity between two influential Arab states, Saudi Arabia and Egypt. Dr. Badeeb argues that for Egypt, the war constituted a means of intensifying and confirming its role as the leader of the revolutionary camp in the Arab world. For Saudi Arabia, however, it presented a direct challenge to the security and stability of the kingdom. Dr. Badeeb provides a valuable elucidation of Saudi Arabia's concern over Yemen as a potential source of political and strategic upheaval. This largely unappreciated aspect of the regional security picture is in part a legacy of the Saudi-Egyptian conflict of the 1960s and is one of the central elements of current Saudi security policy.

Saeed M. Badeeb was born in Jeddah, Saudi Arabia. After earning a B.A. in 1971 and an M.A. in 1975 from the University of Karachi, Pakistan, in 1983 he received a Master of Philosophy degree and in 1985 a Ph.D. from The George Washington University. His fields of specialization were International Relations and Comparative Government and Politics. From 1972 to 1975 Badeeb served as First Secretary of the Saudi Government Advisory Council (Royal Court). From 1980 to 1984 he served as a political adviser in the embassy of Saudi Arabia in Washington, D.C. He is currently a deputy minister without portfolio in the government of Saudi Arabia.

The Saudi-Egyptian Conflict over North Yemen, 1962–1970

Saeed M. Badeeb

Foreword by J. E. Peterson

Westview Press • Boulder, Colorado

American-Arab Affairs Council
Washington, D.C.

Copyright © 1986 by the American-Arab Affairs Council

Published in 1986 in the United States of America by Westview Press, Inc., Frederick A. Praeger, Publisher, 5500 Central Avenue, Boulder, Colorado 80301; and by the American-Arab Affairs Council, 1730 M Street, N.W., Suite 512, Washington, D.C. 20036

Library of Congress Cataloging-in-Publication Data
Badeeb, Saeed M.
  The Saudi-Egyptian conflict over North Yemen,
1962–1970.
  Includes bibliographies and index.
  1. Yemen—History—1962– . 2. Egypt—Foreign
relations—Saudi Arabia. 3. Saudi Arabia—Foreign
relations—Egypt. I. Title.
DS247.Y48B22 1986   953'.32   86-19115
ISBN 0-8133-7296-8

Composition for this book was created by conversion of the author's computer tapes or word-processor disks.
This book was produced without formal editing by the publisher.

Printed and bound in the United States of America

The paper used in this publication meets the requirements of the American National Standard for Permanence of Paper for Printed Library Materials Z39.48-1984.

10   9   8   7   6   5   4   3   2   1

To the memory of my father (God rest his soul in peace)

CONTENTS

ix

FOREWORD

Twenty years ago, the young Yemen Arab Republic was emerging from the wreckage of a long, debilitating civil war. The 1960s were the heyday of the Arab Cold War, that titanic struggle between the opposing forces of progressives and conservatives, between radicals and reactionaries. It was principally a bloodless clash of ideological rhetoric between the new, military-dominated republics and the older, more traditional monarchies for the soul of the Arab world.

But the rugged mountains and terraced valleys of far-off Yemen became the Arab world's battlefields by proxy, and the fighting there was as much between Egypt and Saudi Arabia as it was between Yemeni republicans and royalists. The war in Yemen raged on for five hard years until the June 1967 Arab-Israeli war forced Egypt's disengagement. But the process of "national reconciliation" in Yemen was not completed until 1970, and only then could the first foundations of a modern, effective state be established.

One important consequence of the civil war and the subsequent national reconciliation was the creation of an enduring alliance between Saudi Arabia and the YAR. The geographical proximity of these two countries, their conservative outlooks, similar societies and common threat perceptions, the contribution made by many thousands of Yemeni workers to the development of Saudi Arabia and the kingdom's considerable financial assistance to its much poorer neighbor, have all played a role in forging what Dr. Saeed Badeeb has termed "the inevitable partnership."

Dr. Badeeb's study is a valuable contribution for several reasons. First, he has expanded our knowledge about the wider ramifications of the Yemeni civil war, particularly the causes and extent of Egyptian and Saudi involvement. At the same time, the transcript of Dr. Badeeb's interview with the former Imam, Muhammad al-Badr, constitutes a fascinating and rare look at the thinking of one of the principal participants in the events of the 1960s.

Second, Dr. Badeeb presents one of the most detailed accounts of the historical, political, economic and security ties between Saudi Arabia and Yemen in print. While the key importance of the Saudi-Yemeni relationship is widely recognized, its component elements, scope and limits rarely have been analyzed to the extent found in this study.

Third, most studies of Saudi Arabia and Yemen have been written by westerners and therefore inevitably reflect a Western viewpoint. As a Saudi citizen and government official, as well as a recipient of a Ph.D. degree from The George Washington University, Dr. Badeeb is uniquely qualified to offer this scholarly and readable analysis of the evolution and present status of one of Saudi Arabia's key foreign-policy concerns.

This welcome and useful book is bound to leave the reader with the hope that it will be the first of many comparable studies by Saudi and other Gulf Arab authors.

J. E. Peterson
Author of *Yemen: The Search for a Modern State*
Washington, DC
July 1986

ACKNOWLEDGMENTS

There are many who contributed to the completion of this work and who deserve my sincere thanks and gratitude. Among those is H.M. Imam Muhammad al-Badr, who was kind enough to see me twice, answering my questions and writing me a valuable historical document. Others, such as Mr. Mahmoud Riad, and a number of Saudi, Yemeni and American present and ex-officials, who played important roles during the Yemeni crisis, were very helpful and responded thoughtfully to my questions and inquiries. At their request, I have omitted any specific reference to them. I also wish to express my appreciation to the professors from George Washington University who guided my dissertation and to Frederick W. Axelgard of Georgetown University's Center for Strategic and International Studies; Anne Joyce, Director of Publications of the American-Arab Affairs Council; and Joyce Bouvier, the manuscript typist, for their efforts.

During the research for this study I was fortunate to have access to government and private archives and materials which were indispensable for the completion of the work. The individuals who helped to make these materials available to me performed an invaluable service. To all these, and many others who were kind enough to share their expertise and knowledge with me, I would like to say thank you, thank you very much.

Saeed M. Badeeb

The Saudi-Egyptian Conflict over North Yemen, 1962–1970

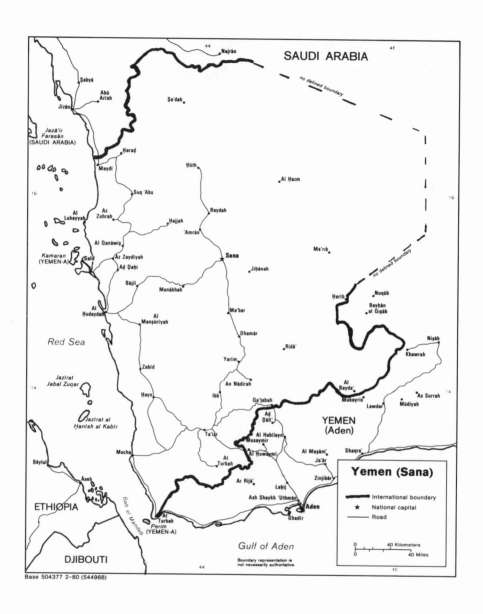

SAUDI ARABIA

Najrān

no defined boundary

Ṣabyā

Abū
ʿArīsh

Jizān

Saʿdah

Jazāʾir
Farasān
(SAUDI ARABIA)

Ḥaraḍ

Maydī

Ḥūth

Al Ḥazm

Suq ʿAbs

Raydah

Az
Zuhrah

Hajjah

ʿAmrān

Maʾrib

Al
Luhayyah

Al Qanāwiṣ

Sana

Jiḥānah

no defined boundary

Kamaran
(YEMEN-A)

Ṣalīf

Az Zaydīyah

Aḍ Ḍaḥi

Bājil

Manākhah

Maʿbar

Ḥarīb

Nuqūb

Bayhān
al Qiṣāb

Al
Ḥudaydah

Al
Manṣūrīyah

Dhamār

Red Sea

Zabīd

Ridāʾ

Niṣāb

Khawrah

Yarīm

Jazirat
Jabal Zuqar

Al
Bayḍāʾ

As Surrah

An Nādirah

Qaʿṭabah

Ḥays

Ibb

Mūkayris

Lawdar

Mūdīyah

Jazirat al
Ḥanīsh al Kabīr

Aḍ
Ḍāliʾ

YEMEN
(Aden)

Bāylul

Taʿizz

Al Ḥabīlayn
Musaymir

Al Maṣāniʿ

Jaʿār

Shaqrāʾ

 Āseb

Al Ḥuwaymi

ETHIꝊPIA

Mocha

At
Turbah

Ar Rijāʾ

Laḥij

Zinjībār

Bāb el Mandeb

Ash Shaykh ʿUthmān

Aden

Yemen (Sana)

━━━ International boundary

★ National capital

─── Road

At
Turbah
Perim
(YEMEN-A)

Ghadir

DJIBOUTI

Gulf of Aden

Boundary representation is
not necessarily authoritative.

0   40 Kilometers
0   40 Miles

Base 504377 2-80 (544968)

Chapter 1

BACKGROUND TO THE REVOLUTION

The Yemen Arab Republic (Y.A.R.), or North Yemen, lies along the southeastern shore of the Red Sea and stretches inland toward the Rub al-Khali desert, north to the Arabian highlands of Saudi Arabia, and south to the People's Democratic Republic of Yemen (P.D.R.Y.), or South Yemen. The P.D.R.Y. commands the Red Sea's southern entrance, the Bab Al-Mandab Strait. This strait has been a principal source of Yemen's regional political importance for over 2,000 years.

During the 16th and 17th centuries, parts of North Yemen were controlled by the Ottoman Empire and then again from 1872 through the end of World War I. For most of the last thousand years, Yemen was ruled by a Zaydi Imam, except during periods of foreign occupation. The Zaydi Imamate system, which existed in Southern Arabia as early as 897 A.D., eventually disappeared from the Peninsula in all but the portion later known as North Yemen.[1] One possible reason for its disappearance is that in claiming descent from Zayd, a son of Ali, son-in-law of the Prophet, the Imams are Shia, whereas Sunnism prevails in most other areas of the Peninsula.

North Yemen is divided nearly evenly into Islamic sects: the Zaydis, a Shia subsect, inhabit the mountains of the north; the Shafis, a branch of Sunnism, are found mainly in the south, along the coast and in neighboring South Yemen. The Zaydi tribes of the northern mountains are loosely grouped into two confederations, the Hashid and the Bakil. Such divisions in the country present both a social and a security issue.[2] During the civil war, the northern Zaydi tribes, who were traditionally aligned with the government, supported the royalists. In contrast, the southern tribes, Shafis and traditionally outsiders, supported the republican forces. In addition, the fact that the society is organized along tribal lines presents a major problem for the central government, which

1

attempts to encourage a common sense of national identity which transcends tribal and sectarian loyalties.[3]

Yemen was last united by Imam Yahya, of the Hamid al-Din family of past Imams, who succeeded his father, al-Mansur Muhammad, in 1904. By shrewdly exploiting the factionalism which characterizes Yemen, taking hostages and using both bribery and intimidation, Yahya succeeded in uniting the country and consolidating his power.[4] After the Turkish defeat in World War I, Imam Yahya gradually assumed both temporal and spiritual control of all of North Yemen. In the process, he established Yemen's first rudimentary central administration and divided the country into six governorships. This tactic helped the state to gain some control over the tribes and villages. Distrusting everyone, however, Imam Yahya gave his governors no power, reserving all authority to himself. Isolationist and xenophobic, he was assassinated in 1948 by Ali al-Qardaci, shaykh of the Murad tribe.[5]

Upon Yahya's death, Abdallah ibn Ahmad al-Wazir, head of a rival family of past Imams, succeeded in getting himself named Imam. A month-long battle for control of the throne followed, with Imam Yahya's son, Ahmad, eventually being victorious. Not wishing to take any chances, Imam Ahmad promptly had many of his rivals executed and others imprisoned.[6] During his reign (Imam Ahmad remained in office until his death in 1962), he continued most of his father's domestic policies. In foreign affairs, however, he showed some willingness to abandon his father's policy of virtually complete isolationism and to venture into official contracts with other countries.

In 1951, Imam Ahmad negotiated a treaty designed to improve relations with the British rulers of Aden. Because of unsettled territorial questions between Sanaa and Aden, the treaty failed to achieve its purpose.[7] Deviating from Yemen's traditional alignment with Saudi Arabia on foreign policy issues, Ahmad also opened relations with the U.S.S.R., recognized the People's Republic of China, and acquired closer ties to Egypt. In 1956, he sent his son, the crown prince, on a visit to the Soviet bloc in search of financial and military aid.[8] Still later, Ahmad himself visited Saudi Arabia, where he signed the Jeddah Military Pact with King Saud and President Nasser.[9] In 1958, Yemen joined with Egypt and Syria to form the United Arab States.[10]

Under Ahmad, Yemen also expanded its contacts with the United States, with which it had signed a friendship and commercial agreement in 1946.[11] In 1957, the chairman of the U.S. House of Representatives Foreign Affairs Committee arrived in Sanaa at the head of a delegation charged with explaining and promoting the Eisenhower Doctrine. Ahmad rejected the doctrine because he did not want to publicly associate himself with a policy aimed at—according to his view—buying Arab support against the U.S.S.R. (communism). However, an American economic mission which presented itself as being unconnected to the Eisenhower Doctrine arrived in Sanaa in September 1957 to do a feasibility study of possible aid prospects.[12] The mission produced a study, but nothing concrete came of it, apparently because of Imam Ahmad's personal distrust of Americans and the United States' lack of interest in Yemen.

The limited progress that Imam Ahmad was able to achieve in social and political affairs was soon brought to an abrupt halt. An unsuccessful coup attempt in 1955 led by his brother, Abdallah, and supported by Colonel Ahmed al-Thalaya, prompted Imam Ahmad in part to rethink his policies. Because he was not a radical innovator, the Imam's modernizing goals and the means used to implement them proved too little, too late, for some of those in the emerging society he governed. The coup attempt, as a rejection of his policies, manifested just how far the struggle between modernity and traditionalism had progressed.[13]

One outcome of the coup was Imam Ahmad's revision of his regional policies. Soon thereafter, he became hostile toward Nasser. Nasser by that time had begun openly promoting his Pan-Arab philosophy and his socialist policies, both of which the Imam regarded as un-Islamic and threatening to his regime. Undoubtedly, he sensed that even if Nasser's speeches were not directly aimed at his overthrow, the relentlessness of the calls for changes, at least partially, had inspired the coup attempt against him. Despite his hostility toward Nasser (and in some ways, because of it), the Imam joined Egypt and Syria in forming the United Arab States in 1958, explaining to Saudi Arabia's King Saud that joining the U.A.S. was the best way to avoid becoming a target of Nasser's propaganda.[14] Not long after Syria's September 1961 withdrawal from the U.A.S., the Imam wrote a poem criticizing socialism and those who nationalize the property of people and those who permit what Islam had prohibited (an oblique reference to the nationalization of property). The poem so angered Nasser that he terminated the confederation in September of 1961.[15]

The Coup and Its Aftermath

Ahmad died of natural causes on September 19, 1962. The rule of his successor, his son Imam Muhammad al-Badr, lasted only eight days. On September 26, 1962, a partially successful coup, led by a Yemen junior Army officer, forced al-Badr to flee from his capital and triggered the events that eventually led to civil war. That night's events, described in Imam al-Badr's own words, were as follows:

On the evening of the coup d'état, I was presiding over the new Council of Ministers located inside the Royal Palace. The meeting ended late at night because many affairs and subjects had to be discussed. While I was walking toward the residential quarter of the palace, an officer called Hussein al-Sukary, who was a deputy to Colonel Abdallah al-Sallal in providing security for the royal palace, tried to assassinate me from behind, but the rifle's trigger jammed. While my personal guards tried to arrest him, he shot himself in the chin. He is still alive today, but with a disfigured face. Al-Sallal, himself, was neither in the meeting of the council nor in the palace at the time. I continued my way towards the residential palace. After resting awhile, the electricity was cut off, and I felt that something wrong was going on. This was followed by gunfire on the palace. I then began with my personal guards and the guards of the palace to fire back. In fact, the ringleader of the coup and its principal Yemeni leader was an officer called Abd al-Ghani who was killed during the early hours of the coup. It is possible that he was the one who had constant contact with the Egyptian Embassy in Sanaa. The death of the Yemeni head plotter and the rumors that the Imam was also killed provided the opportunity for Colonel Abdallah al-Sallal to take over. Al-Sallal, himself, was a long time confidant of mine, whom I appointed Commander of the Royal Guard.[16]

Before the repercussions had ended from the coup d'état which removed Imam Muhammad al-Badr from power, much more had been affected than the destiny of one ruler. His fall from power and the government takeover by republican forces was followed by Egyptian intervention to secure the republican victory. This intervention, in turn, triggered Saudi Arabian participation in the form of political and financial assistance on the side of the deposed Imam. The conflicts of varying interests— Yemeni royalist, Yemeni republican, pro-republican Egypt and Saudi Arabia pro-royalist—ultimately led to a bloody civil war that lasted eight years and transformed a local problem into an international issue. Moreover, as their involvement deepened, Saudi Arabia and Egypt became engaged in what was an undeclared state of war, producing one of the most complex problems to face the Arab world in the 1960s. The deepening divisions between Saudi Arabia and Egypt over their respective roles in the conflict soon had the other Arab states taking sides, contributed to a general state of unrest among the Arab states, and created an ideological spectrum in which Arab countries became classified as nationalists, imperialists, radicals, conservatives, and moderates. This "side-taking" thereby broadened the scope of the Yemeni conflict so that it engulfed both the conservative and revolutionary Arab camps, with Saudi Arabia leading the conservatives and Egypt leading the revolutionaries.

The conflict, which lasted from 1962–1970, was resolved only when the Yemenis themselves opted to decide their fate alone and without further outside influence. Before that happened, however, the reach of the Yemeni Civil War had extended far beyond the original players and their partisans and had affected even the superpowers. It involved the United States as a mediator to cool the tensions between Saudi Arabia and Egypt and as an executor of limited military operations on the side of the Saudis. The U.S.S.R.'s involvement cast it as a supporter of Egypt's Gamal Abd al-Nasser, encouraging his continued participation in the conflict, and later supplying military and technical aid to the republican forces. Finally, the impact of the war and the Saudi-Egyptian conflict expanded to include even more participants—from other Arab states to regional and international organizations.

Significance of the Issue

The consequences of the Yemeni Civil War are with us today in the form of continuing border disputes and negotiations between North Yemen and Saudi Arabia. Aside from this, the civil war must be regarded as a watershed in that it presaged a new political era in the Arab world and in the relations of the powers within the region. The Yemeni Civil War also represented a major issue in the superpowers' rivalry over the Third World and the Middle East.

In the chapters that follow, we will examine the internal and external factors within Yemen which determined the course of events in that country both prior to and following the 1962 coup d'état and the ensuing civil war. This will include a survey of the internal situation existing in North Yemen prior to the coup in order to develop an understanding both of the reasons behind it and of the character of the groups which opposed and supported it.

A second major purpose of this work is to trace the historical development of the Saudi-Egyptian conflict over North Yemen. This task requires an understanding of the relations among these outside parties at the time of the 1962 coup as well as the political and military relations which had existed among them up to that time.

A third basic objective of this study is to treat, for the first time, the Saudi perception of North Yemen. Analyzing and examining this issue will clarify the seemingly vague Saudi role in the conflict and will shed new light on the nature of Saudi Arabia's economic, political and military assistance to North Yemen. As a source of new information on the role of one of the important players in this conflict and as a guide to present-day Saudi-Yemeni relations, it is hoped that this work will prove a useful contribution to the literature on this area.

Finally, underlying all of these thrusts is the question of how a "simple" coup d'état in a remote area of the world evolved into a regional crisis of significant proportions and triggered the involvement of regional and international organizations, and ultimately the superpowers themselves.

Notes

[1] William R. Brown, "The Yemeni Dilemma," *The Middle East Journal*, vol. 17, no. 4 (Autumn 1963), p. 349.

[2] David McClintock, "The Yemen Arab Republic" in David Long and Bernard Reich, eds., *The Government and Politics of the Middle East and North Africa* (Boulder, CO: Westview Press, 1980), p. 176.

[3] J. E. Peterson, *Yemen: The Search for a Modern State* (Baltimore: The Johns Hopkins University Press, 1982), p. 172.

[4] Edgar O'Ballance, *The War in Yemen* (London: Faber and Faber, 1971), p. 26.

[5] Although Yemen, under Yahya's leadership, joined both the Arab League in 1945 and the United Nations in 1948, Yahya refused to allow foreign diplomats to live in Yemen. At the time of his death, he had only one ambassador abroad (in Cairo). O'Ballance, p. 26. Al-Gardai was executed later that same year. Robert Stookey, *Yemen: The Politics of the Yemen Arab Republic* (Boulder, CO: Westview Press, 1978), p. 179.

[6] Jane Smiley Hart, "Basic Chronology for a History of the Yemen," *The Middle East Journal*, vol. 17, nos. 1 and 2 (Winter and Spring 1963), p. 149.

[7] George Lenczowski, *The Middle East in World Affairs*, 4th ed. (Ithaca: Cornell University Press, 1980), p. 617.

[8] H.M. Imam al-Badr affirmed in an interview that he was responsible for bringing the Russians into Yemen. See Appendix No. 2, Question and Answer Number 12.

[9] Mohammed Ahmed Zabarah, *Yemen: Tradition vs. Modernity* (New York: Praeger, 1982), p. 56.

[10] There is some evidence to suggest that Ahmad joined the U.A.S. in order to avoid becoming a target of Nasser's propaganda. Lenczowski, p. 623. H.E. Mahmoud Riad, Egypt's Ambassador to Syria from 1954–1958, told the author that Egypt had proposed a five-year plan for unity with Syria. The Syrians, however, insisted on immediate union. Therefore, when Imam Ahmad decided to join the union, President Nasser had little choice but to agree. Appendix No. 4, Question and Answer Number 1.

[11] See text of agreement, Appendix No. 3.

[12] Eric Macro, *Yemen and the Western World* (New York: Frederick A. Praeger Publishers, 1968), pp. 122–123.

[13] Zabarah, p. 63.

[14] Christopher J. McMullen, *Resolution of the Yemen Crisis 1963: A Case Study in Mediation* (Washington, DC: Institute for the Study of Diplomacy,

School of Foreign Service, Georgetown University, 1980), p. 26. See also footnote 10, above.

[15] Zabarah, p. 63.

[16] See text of interview, Appendix No. 2, Question and Answer Number 4. See also, O'Ballance, p. 67.

Chapter 2

HISTORICAL BACKGROUND OF POLITICAL AND MILITARY RELATIONS AMONG SAUDI ARABIA, YEMEN AND EGYPT, 1932 TO 1962

Historical factors going back to the 1930s complicate the political and military relations existing among Saudi Arabia, Yemen and Egypt. These factors include the bonds that unite these countries, namely ethnicity, religion and language. Saudi Arabia, Yemen and Egypt belong to the Arab nation, share the Islamic faith and speak the Arabic language. In addition, though they eventually developed very different political systems, they all shared a common monarchial form of government at the beginning of the 1930s. But over the three decades under consideration here, close ties between three politically similar regimes disintegrated into open hostility between radically different governments and ideologies. By the early 1960s, Egypt and Saudi Arabia found themselves heavily involved in a proxy war for the future political orientation of Yemen and even for the soul of the Arab world.

Political Relations

Political relations among Saudi Arabia, Yemen and Egypt from 1932 to 1962 ranged from very good to indifferent to complete rupture. At the same time, meaningful comparisons and contrasts can be made in the relations existing between Saudi Arabia and Egypt on the one hand and between Saudi Arabia and Yemen on the other.

The first similarity which can be discerned about Saudi Arabia's relations with Egypt and Yemen stems from Abd al-Aziz's creation of the Kingdom of Saudi Arabia in 1932. For similar reasons, specifically their objections to King Abd al-Aziz's annexation of certain provinces, both Egypt and Yemen refused to recognize Abd al-Aziz's claims to kingship.[1]

Egypt objected to King Abd al-Aziz's 1924 acquisition of the Hejaz and its holy cities of Makkah (Mecca) and Medina.[2] An ambitious King Fouad of Egypt wished to establish Cairo as the capital of Islam and himself as caliph. His ambition, coupled with jealousy and traditional Egyptian hatred of the zealous Wahhabis, led to a break in relations between Riyadh and Cairo between 1929 and 1936.[3] This break was triggered by Fouad's refusal to recognize the Saudi Arabian political agency which had been headquartered in Cairo since 1925. By 1929, Fouad's refusal had exhausted King Abd al-Aziz's patience and prompted him to demand the closing of the Egyptian political agency which was located in Jeddah. Relations between the two countries were eventually resumed in 1936, when a new king, Faruq, assumed the Egyptian throne. At that time, the Egyptian Guardianship Council approved the restoration of diplomatic relations with Saudi Arabia. On May 7, 1936, the two countries signed a treaty of mutual understanding in which Egypt fully recognized Saudi Arabia's independence and sovereignty.[4] However, until that came about, bringing with it a change in the atmosphere surrounding the dealings between the two countries, relations between them were filled with mistrust and misunderstanding.

Yemeni-Saudi relations also were troubled by Saudi territorial expansion. Yemen's leader, Imam Yahya, objected to King Abd al-Aziz's claim to sovereignty over the province of Asir, including the two cities of Najran and Jizan. King Abd al-Aziz based his 1931 claim to these cities on a 1926 agreement between him and the Asir's ruler, al-Idrisi, under which Asir came under Saudi protection.[5] Al-Idrisi repudiated this agreement in 1931, and King Abd al-Aziz promptly occupied Asir. The king's action provoked the Yemeni Imam and prompted him to press his claim to the area.

As a result, Yemen did not recognize King Abd al-Aziz's sovereignty and pursued negotiations over the province during 1932–1934. When the negotiations stalled over the Imam's insistence on annexing Najran, King Abd al-Aziz prodded the Imam first by issuing a warning and then, when Yahya sent his troops to Najran, by conquering the Yemeni port of al-Hudaydah.[6] King Abd al-Aziz's demonstration of strength accomplished its purpose and the Imam returned to the negotiating table. In May, the Taif Treaty of 1934 was signed. It included a Pact of Arbitration, valid for 20 years, and the treaty was subject to prolongation or abrogation upon either party's giving notice six months before the 20-year period ended. The treaty and its pact continued in force, undisturbed, extending itself automatically for the next 28 years. The Pact of Arbitration was not invoked until 1962.[7]

In summary, while Egypt and Yemen were initially offended by the new borders of Saudi Arabia, both countries undertook positive relations that began with the signing of bilateral treaties with the new kingdom: Egypt in 1936 and Yemen in 1934. Particular note should be made here as well of the contribution King Abd al-Aziz made to fostering better relations between Saudi Arabia, Egypt and Yemen. His pragmatism and common sense contributed significantly to the success of the peace negotiations with Yemen and to the establishment of diplomatic relations with Egypt. Despite his victory at al-Hudaydah, King Abd al-Aziz was willing to re-enter negotiations with Yemen. When Egypt's Guardianship Council approached him, he responded without hesitation.

Egyptian-Saudi Relations

Relations between Saudi Arabia and Egypt improved significantly with King Faruq's accession to the Egyptian throne in 1936. In great part, this improvement can be traced to the way in which King Abd al-Aziz responded to the Egyptian call for forming the Arab League. In fact, relations between the two monarchies from 1936 to 1943 could be described as good and steadily improving. When the Arab League issue was first raised, King Abd al-Aziz was reluctant to participate in the talks, which had been called for on March 31, 1943, by Egypt's Premier Mustafa al-Nahhas. King Abd al-Aziz's reluctance was based on his knowledge that the British were behind Nahhas's call. The idea of forming an Arab League was first mentioned by Anthony Eden, the British foreign minister, in an address given in 1943 at Guild Hall in London. However, the king's reluctance was eventually overcome by the efforts of the Egyptian government and the personal entreaty of King Faruq, who appealed to the cause of Arab unity.[8] By the time the final signature was put on the Arab League Charter in Cairo on March 22, 1945, the beginnings of a friendship between the two sovereigns was evident, and the relationship was further cemented when the Egyptian sovereign arrived at the port of Yanbu in Saudi Arabia on December 27, 1945.

King Faruq's visit was a success, with King Abd al-Aziz personally meeting and welcoming his visitor upon his arrival. Soon after, King Abd al-Aziz accepted King Faruq's invitation to visit Egypt. That trip occurred on January 10, 1947. By then, cordial relations between the two kings had been firmly established. Their talks included bilateral relations as well as their relations with Britain. Despite his differences with Britain over the Buraimi Oasis, King Abd al-Aziz advised King

Faruq to reach a settlement of the dispute over British occupation of the Suez Canal Zone.[9] The tone of the Saudi monarch's visit and of overall Egyptian-Saudi relations at the time was described by the late President Anwar al-Sadat in the following words:

> . . . indeed, the whole country had been preparing for it for a long time. The late King Saud [Abd al-Aziz ibn Saud] was a noble and generous hero. He had proved quite hospitable during King Farouq's visit to Saudi Arabia and the latter wanted to return his hospitality. Above all, King Saud loved Egypt. The Saudi ruling family's love for Egypt is traditional, and each monarch is always careful to maintain good and close relations with Egypt.[10]

The warm relations between Egypt and Saudi Arabia continued to develop until July 23, 1952, when the Egyptian coup d'état ended monarchial rule in Egypt.[11] Neither the internal military struggle which continued in that country until Nasser assumed power in March 1954, nor the death of King Abd al-Aziz on November 9, 1952, affected the cordial relations between the countries.

Upon King Abd al-Aziz's death, his eldest son, Saud, ascended the Saudi throne. Although King Saud carefully watched Egypt's political struggle, Saudi Arabia remained neutral.[12] When Nasser finally assumed control of Egypt in 1954, King Saud welcomed his leadership and prepared himself for continued close and fruitful relations with that country. The new blood and the new generation of rulers in both countries augmented a good foundation for mutual understanding and for further progress toward mutual cooperation and strong bilateral relations. This feeling, fed by Nasser's charismatic personality, was reinforced during Nasser's first visit to Saudi Arabia in 1954. As Robert Lacey observed,

> Colonel Gamal Abdul Nasser offered the Arab World a new vision of itself in the 1950s. His intoxicating blend of nationalism and radicalism set the Middle East alight with pride, ambition and an excitement the Arabs had not experienced for centuries.
>
> Nasser had extraordinary personal presence. He was a tall man, broad and beefy like a boxer, with flashing eyes and a prodigious smile, and when he first came to Saudi Arabia in 1954 King Saud embraced him as a brother. Nasser came to Makkah to do his pilgrimage and to request Saudi partnership in his crusade to unite the Arab World and the new King Saud responded warmly.[13]

After Nasser's visit, relations between Saudi Arabia and Egypt took on a new shape and substance. Tangible effects included the arrival of a 200-person Egyptian military mission in January, 1955, to train the Saudi army; the arrival of Egyptian advisors to set up the bureaucratic procedures of Saudi Arabia's civil service; and the arrival of Egyptian teachers to staff the kingdom's new schools.[14]

In addition to these concrete manifestations of closer relations between the two countries, Nasser succeeded in obtaining Saudi support for his new policies. This included support for the policy of non-alignment and King Saud's participation in a joint denunciation of the Baghdad Pact, a British sponsored, pro-Western military alliance. Moreover, during King Saud's visit to Cairo in the spring of 1956, the king and Nasser conferred on Nasser's proposal to bring Egypt, Syria and Saudi Arabia together in a grand, three-cornered union. Although King Saud would not go as far as union with Egypt and Syria, he agreed to finance a tripartite alliance and to stand by both countries in peace and war. This alliance was designed to counter Western influence in the area, as evidenced by the Baghdad Pact. The members of the alliance were motivated by a desire to identify themselves as part of a new category of countries—the non-aligned—rather than by antipathy for any particular country.[15]

By late 1955, however, the relationship between King Saud and Nasser, which had started off so auspiciously, began to sour. At that time, Egyptian broadcasts on Cairo Radio began advocating Arab socialism. Nevertheless, although King Saud's suspicions of Nasser's ultimate intentions were aroused, King Saud continued to pursue cordial relations, albeit more cautiously than before. Perhaps he believed that being close to Nasser was still preferable to being alienated from him. King Saud's suspicions were strengthened, however, when, in July 1956, President Nasser announced the nationalization of the Suez Canal, an unprecedented move which had been taken without having either consulted or informed King Saud beforehand of his intentions. Yet, despite any displeasure King Saud might have felt as a result of President Nasser's unilateral action, he did not object. In fact, when Nasser flew to Saudi Arabia two months later, King Saud offered him both political and military cooperation.[16]

The French, British, and Israeli tripartite attack on Egypt in November 1956 followed King Saud's offer by only a few days. Saudi Arabia responded by offering Egypt use of its airfields and by ordering Aramco to cease oil sales to Britain and France.[17] Despite its faithful gesture, at the war's end King Saud felt that Saudi Arabia's contribution had been ignored, as Nasser took full credit for the war and its successful conclusion. Nasser's popularity soared, as did his confidence in his personal ability to influence events and agitate for changes throughout the Arab world. King Saud's wariness of Nasser's intentions had increased and the honeymoon which had existed between the two came to an end. Political relations between the two countries rapidly deteriorated, and in 1957 Nasser launched a violent propaganda campaign against the House of Saud. To wit, Nasser began supporting an Arab "revolution" that aimed at the overthrow of the conservative regimes in the Arab world and the creation of a single Arab nation. To further his goal, particularly *vis-à-vis* Saudi Arabia, Nasser allowed radical groups such as the Arabian Peninsula People's Union (APPU), an anti-Saudi movement headed by Nasir al-Said, to operate from Egypt.[18]

Nasser's campaign against the king came in retaliation for King Saud's disclosure of an Egyptian-backed plot to assassinate him and the arrest of an Egyptian servant charged by Saudi intelligence with planting a bomb in the king's bedroom.[19] According to H.E. Mahmoud Riad, Egypt's foreign minister in 1964 and later during 1967–1971, the "plot" in actuality was a C.I.A. (Central Intelligence Agency) ruse designed to embitter relations between Egypt and Saudi Arabia. Mr. Riad subsequently charged that the C.I.A. planned the operation and passed details of the supposed plot through Syrian President Shukri al-Quwatli. He believed that, even then, the United States wanted to isolate Egypt from the Arab world in order to secure Israel's existence, something he said was finally accomplished by the 1979 Camp David Accords.[20] Nevertheless, Mr. Riad's view represents his own perception, which can neither be denied nor confirmed. However, the assassination attempt was confirmed by a highly placed, reliable Saudi official.[21]

The poor relations which then existed between the two countries were exacerbated when, on February 22, 1958, Egypt and Syria declared their official union in the United Arab Republic (U.A.R.) and named Nasser its president. King Saud worried that the union of the two countries might presage a threat to Saudi borders, and, at the very least, he feared an increased threat to Saudi Arabia's security and stability. Despite these concerns, King Saud did not believe the union could survive for long. His beliefs in this regard were shared by his brother, Crown Prince Faisal. In his autobiography, the late President Sadat, then deputy speaker of the Eygptian Presidential Council, recounted a conversation he had with the Crown Prince in Cairo a few days before the unity agreement was signed:

> Faisal: The union won't survive—it won't fit in with the political current over there [meaning Syria] and will do you harm. . . . You will be dealt a blow in the end.
>
> Sadat: It is all over, Faisal. Al-Kuatli will be here in two days' time for the union to be officially declared—the decision is irreversible.

> Faisal: I'm telling you this just to clear my conscience. You can be sure this union will end in disaster.[22]

Crown Prince Faisal's assessment of the union's chances for success was predicated upon his full knowledge of Syria's being a tribalist and fractionalized country. His beliefs and those of the king were proved correct when the union collapsed in July 1961.

Though the union disintegrated before it could threaten Saudi Arabia, it was little more than a year after its 1961 collapse that King Saud's fears of a border threat were realized and Egypt actually did threaten Saudi Arabia's territory. Needless to say, it was then that Saudi-Egyptian relations reached their lowest point. In September 1962 Egypt intervened militarily in North Yemen.

Saudi-Yemeni Relations

As previously discussed, the tension which existed in Saudi-Yemeni relations subsided with the conclusion of the 1934 Treaty of Taif and set the stage for good future relations. The intentions of the two rulers are set forth in Article I of the treaty, which states that:

> . . . a permanent state of peace, close friendship, and a permanent Islamic and Arabic brotherhood, will be established between the two kings and their nations, that cannot be interrupted partly or totally. . . . They both make Almighty God a witness of their good will and their sincere wish for conciliation and agreement secretly and publicly.[23]

In addition to the Treaty of Taif, several other factors contributed to the development of good relations between the two countries during this period. First, although Imam Yahya had established a state designed to uphold traditional values, he was backed as its ruler by a nascent central government.[24] He therefore had a good deal of incentive to settle his disputes with his neighbors in order to give him the freedom he needed to attend to internal matters of state. Second, King Abd al-Aziz had a good deal of incentive to settle his disputes as well. Having recently established the Kingdom of Saudi Arabia, he was anxious to secure its borders and establish friendly relations with his neighbors. As in the case of Imam Yahya, such freedom from outside concerns would enable the newly established ruler to devote himself to governing his people and attending to affairs of state. Third, from a practical standpoint, Imam Yahya had every tangible reason for wanting to maintain good relations with Saudi Arabia because he recognized Ibn Saud's military superiority. In 1934, when negotiations stalled over the disputed territories in Asir, Yahya had been treated to an impressive demonstration of Ibn Saud's superior military strength. Prince Faisal's military occupation of North Yemen's Red Sea coast up to and including the port of al-Hudaydah had taught the Imam to respect the strength of his northern neighbor. Imam Yahya's subsequent return to the negotiating table and the successful conclusion of the Treaty of Taif clearly reveals that he recognized the advisability of maintaining good relations with Ibn Saud.

The improved relations between Saudi Arabia and Yemen in the post-1934 period were strong enough to survive a number of potential political crises, including an unsuccessful attempt to assassinate the Saudi ruler. If there had been less trust between the two leaders, the fact that two of the would-be assassins were members of the Yemeni army might have resulted in the levelling of charges of government complicity before an investigation of the facts could take place. During the 1935 *hajj* (pilgrimage) season, King Abd al-Aziz and Crown Prince Saud were performing their religious duties inside Makkah's Grand Mosque when they were attacked by three Yemenis wielding daggers.[25] Two of the attackers were killed during the ensuing struggle with the king's bodyguards; a third died of his injuries an hour later. Before the third attacker died, however, he admitted to Saudi authorities that he and his two accomplices had intended to kill both the king and the crown prince. An investigation undertaken soon afterwards revealed that these men had acted alone. The investigation further disclosed that not only had there been no organized plot, but there had been no awareness of it of any kind on the part of the Imam's government, notwithstanding the fact that two of the attackers were members of the Yemeni armed forces.[26] The goodwill existing between Saudi Arabia and Yemen was further enhanced in March 1937 when Yemen became the third member to join a friendship pact initially agreed to by Saudi Arabia and Iraq on April 2, 1936. This pact merits special note because it was unique in several respects: it was signed by the only states in the Arab world to have achieved their independence at that time; it covered manifold aspects of relations among the three countries, including criminal laws, political and economic matters, territorial conflicts, religious and cultural matters and military cooperation; and it included a forward-looking provision which permitted any Arab state gaining its independence in the future to become a party to the pact.[27]

The 1934 treaty, which settled the territorial dispute between Saudi Arabia and Yemen, and the 1937 agreement, which provided for coordination between them on a variety of matters, made it possible for the two countries to enjoy close and cordial political relations. The litmus test of these positive relations came in the aftermath of the 1948 assassination of Imam Yahya.

The 1948 Assassination and Coup

In the wake of the February 17, 1948, assassination of Imam Yahya, Abdallah al-Wazir, former adviser to the Imam and a prominent member of one of Yemen's aristocratic families, seized control of the government and thereby deprived the Imam's son and appointed successor, Ahmad, of his throne.[28] Seeking to legitimize his takeover, al-Wazir asked King Abd al-Aziz to recognize him as the legitimate ruler of Yemen. In keeping with his policies, which were aimed at stabilizing the Arabian Peninsula while repudiating violence and upholding agreements, King Abd al-Aziz condemned the assassination and takeover and eschewed al-Wazir's request for recognition. In sharp contrast to his treatment of al-Wazir, King Abd al-Aziz offered Imam Ahmad his moral support and congratulations when, with the help of Yemen's Zaydi tribes, Ahmad was able to crush al-Wazir's movement and regain his crown.[29] As a sign of appreciation for King Abd al-Aziz's support, Imam Ahmad thereafter aligned himself politically with Saudi Arabia in foreign policy matters.

The Imam continued to support the foreign-policy initiatives of Saudi Arabia until King Abd al-Aziz's death in 1953. For example, when Saudi Arabia decided to be legally neutral towards the 1952 revolution in Egypt, Yemen followed suit. In 1956, Imam Ahmad travelled to Saudi Arabia to join King Saud and President Nasser in signing the Jeddah Pact. In addition, both countries supported Arab causes, such as the Palestinian question, and condemned the 1956 tripartite attack on Egypt. Thereafter, although the divergent interests of Yemen and Saudi Arabia led Imam Ahmad to pursue an independent foreign policy line, the cordial relations between the two countries continued as before. These divergent interests were exemplified by Yemen's joining the 1958 union between Syria and Egypt, an action that Saudi Arabia did not support.

The Imam's new foreign-policy direction, while not totally at odds with Saudi Arabia's, used previously untried channels to put an end to Yemen's isolationist stance and secure its interests in the world arena. In pursuit of these objectives, Imam Ahmad achieved a rapprochement with the Soviet Union and its allies, recognized the People's Republic of China, and sought close ties with Nasser's Egypt.[30] Despite these moves, Saudi Arabia continued to coordinate itself politically with Yemen and to support the Imamate as the legitimate source of power in that country. Saudi Arabia's loyalty to the Imamate was tested for the second time in 1955 when Yemen was threatened by another attempted coup d'état.

The Abortive 1955 Coup Attempt

Unlike the 1948 coup d'état, the 1955 coup attempt was largely a family affair. Rather than replace the Imamate system, the plotters sought to have Ahmad, the ruling Imam, step down in favor of his brother Abdallah. The plotters, who wanted to increase the pace of modernization in Yemen, believed that they would more easily accomplish their aims under Abdallah than under Ahmad.[31]

In March 1955, Colonel Ahmad al-Thalaya, inspector-general of the army, succeeded in besieging Imam Ahmad in his Taiz palace and procured an ambiguous letter of abdication from the Imam. Ahmad's brother, Abdallah, took advantage of the opportunity to have himself named Imam and then appointed his brother, Abbas, as prime minister. Imam Ahmad's son, Crown Prince Muhammad al-Badr, was out of the country when he learned of the coup. His presence outside Yemen permitted him to launch a diplomatic campaign aimed at regaining his father's throne. After first contacting Saudi Arabia, Egypt and the Arab League in search of support, al-Badr entered Yemen and began to gather forces to free Imam Ahmad. From Yemen, al-Badr sent a delegation to Saudi Arabia requesting military assistance in his attempt to unseat Abdallah.[32] King Saud quickly agreed to help al-Badr, but before the Saudi monarch was able to carry out his promise, Imam Ahmad himself had regained his throne. Acting on his own, Imam Ahmad, who was well known throughout Yemen and Arabia for his prowess and courage, unseated his brother and won the rebels over to his side,[33] thus obviating the need for Saudi Arabia to carry out its commitment to support militarily the Imam and his son, the Crown Prince.

Saudi-Yemeni relations continued to improve in 1956 and 1957. Imam Ahmad ventured beyond Yemeni borders for a rare occasion when he visited Saudi Arabia in April 1956 and was met by King Saud in Jeddah. On the following day, they were joined by President Gamal Abd al-Nasser of Egypt, and the three leaders then signed the Jeddah Military Pact.[34] (In 1962, this pact was used by Egypt to justify its intervention in Yemen.) Later in 1956, Saudi Arabia's first ambassador to Yemen presented his credentials to Imam Ahmad. Prior to that time, the two countries had conducted their relations through the exchange of *ad hoc* and temporary task-oriented missions on an issue-to-issue basis. Fruitful relations and mutual understanding continued to characterize relations between the two countries throughout 1957 and until Yemen's 1958 decision to join Egypt and Syria in forming the United Arab States (U.A.S.).

Before Yemen's decision to join the U.A.S. was finalized, King Saud did his best to dissuade Imam Ahmad from the union. The Imam refused to be swayed, however, and instead insisted that joining the U.A.S. was the best way to avoid becoming a target of Nasser's propaganda.[35] The union took place in 1958, and relations between Saudi Arabia and Yemen were impaired as a consequence, with each country pursuing its own—and often conflicting—foreign policy line. For example, during the 1950s, Yemen's closer relations with the Soviet Union and its alignment with Nasser made it politically difficult for Saudi Arabia to pursue closer ties with Yemen. The deterioration in relations between Saudi Arabia and Yemen continued until 1961, when the union between Egypt, Syria and Yemen collapsed. With the dismemberment of the United Arab States, cordial relations between Saudi Arabia and Yemen were again resumed.

The 1962 Coup d'Etat

Imam Ahmad died in bed of natural causes on September 19, 1962. King Saud sent his brother Prince Fahd, then minister of education and later king of Saudi Arabia, to head the Saudi delegation to North Yemen. This delegation, sent both to console the Hamid al-Din family of Yemen and to congratulate the new Imam, Ahmad's son Muhammad al-Badr, represented direct Saudi recognition of the legitimacy of Imamate rule in Yemen. It was also intended as a statement of Saudi Arabia's continuing commitment to its agreements with Yemen, particularly the 1934 Taif Treaty and the 1956 Jeddah Military Pact.[36] But, on September 26, 1962, just one week after Imam Ahmad's death, a successful coup d'état removed Imam al-Badr from power, installed a pro-Egyptian republican regime in its place, and ushered in a new phase in Saudi-Yemeni political and military relations.

Military Relations Among the Three Countries: 1932–1962

The military relations characterizing the three countries between 1932–1962 may best be examined by dividing them into two facets, the first dealing with the negative aspects of those relations and the second dealing with the positive aspects.

Negative Aspects of the Military Relationships

The only negative military incident which occurred between Saudi Arabia and Yemen during this period took place in April 1934. Two years of unsuccessful negotiations over the Asir had created a strain in Saudi-Yemeni relations. These relations were further strained by a series of border violations on the part of both countries. First, farmers on either side of the Saudi-Yemeni border began crossing the border at will in order to graze and water their sheep and camels, thereby increasing tension between the two governments. Second, a number of Yemeni soldiers crossed the Saudi border and, after attacking several Saudi border posts, entered the highlands of Wadi Najran and occupied part of Najran.[37]

The border violations on the part of both the farmers and the soldiers, coupled with the inconclusive negotiations, prompted King Abd al-Aziz to dispatch his two eldest sons to Yemen, and thus touched off a bloody war between the two countries. Prince Saud was sent to the mountainous areas of Najran and Yam, and Prince Faisal went to the coastal areas of Asir. Both sons achieved their goals of recapturing occupied Saudi outposts and putting an end to border violations. Prince Faisal's forces went further, reaching deep inside Yemen to occupy a number of Yemeni towns including the port city of al-Hudaydah far to the south. These Saudi military triumphs frightened Imam Yahya and persuaded him to call for a cease-fire and for the resumption of peace talks. King Abd al-Aziz agreed, and talks were resumed in mid-May 1934 in the Saudi city of al-Taif.[38] Soon after, on May 19, 1934, the two countries concluded an agreement that has become known as the Taif Treaty of 1934.[39] It ended the state of war between the two countries and led to the demarcation of their mutual borders. From then until 1962, the two countries experienced no further military confrontation.

Saudi Arabia and Egypt, on the other hand, never confronted each other militarily during this period. Likewise, Yemen and Egypt never confronted one another militarily between 1932 and 1962. It was not until 1962—after a 28-year peace between Saudi Arabia and Yemen, and for the first time ever between Saudi Arabia and Egypt and between Egypt and Yemen—that these countries raised arms against one another. This confrontation, in Yemen and on the Saudi-Yemeni border, came about as a direct result of the 1962 coup.

Positive Aspects of the Military Relationships

From 1932 to 1962, Saudi Arabia, Egypt and Yemen formed a number of military alignments, cooperated militarily, and entered into several military pacts. These arrangements were significant for two reasons: first, they promoted the parties' understanding of the security issues facing them and enabled them to coordinate their responses to perceived problems and dangers; second, and in a wider context, these arrangements were made by three Arab states at a time when they were still struggling to free themselves of the colonialist influence, itself a benchmark in Arab politics of the 1950s.

The Saudi-Yemeni Pact of 1937. The first of several agreements to be entered into by these countries was the Saudi-Yemeni Pact of 1937.

This pact in fact came as an amendment to an earlier Saudi-Iraqi accord signed on April 2, 1936. That agreement in essence was the first military pact to be signed by Arab states. Article Three provides:

> If a conflict between one of the undersigned parties and another country takes place and leads to a situation where the danger of imminent war could arise, the three parties will then join their efforts to solve the conflict peacefully and through friendly negotiations.

Article Four continues:

> If, after following the procedures outlined in Item Three above, there is nevertheless an attack on one of the Undersigned parties by another country, then the undersigned parties agree to consult each other concerning the measures to be taken with the aim of arriving at a course of action using useful and beneficial means to rebuff the attack. The following acts are to be considered hostile:
>
> (1) Declarations of war.
> (2) The forceful occupation of one of the states party to this pact by another country even if such occupying state did not declare war.
> (3) An attack by another country's land, naval, or air forces against one of the pact members, its ships, or its airplanes, even if the attacker did not declare war.
> (4) Assisting or helping the attacker directly or indirectly.[40]

This pact's importance stems from four factors: (1) it was signed by the three Arab states which had achieved independence at that time; (2) it emphasized tripartite political and military cooperation; (3) it signified the confirmation of both King Abd al-Aziz and Imam Yahya that the 1934 Taif Treaty was still valid and binding and, further, that it was enforceable through the tripartite pact; and, (4) the pact was seen by other Arab countries still operating under varying forms of foreign occupation, colonization and trusteeship, as a move toward "decoupling" Arab policies and military actions from that of the Western powers dominant in the Middle East at that time, namely, Great Britain and France.

Agreements and Alignments of the Mid-1950s. From 1954 through 1956, nearly two decades after the Saudi-Yemeni Pact came into being, a series of other agreements was negotiated which signaled even closer military cooperation between the parties. These included: (1) The Yemeni-Egyptian Mutual Defense Pact of 1954. This agreement, entered into in July 1954, provided for an Egyptian military training mission to be sent to Yemen. Later that year, 14 Egyptian officers arrived in Sanaa and remained there to train Yemeni officers for nearly one year.[41] (2) The Saudi Arabian-Egyptian Mutual Defense Pact of 1954. As a result of this October 1954 agreement, 200 Egyptian military advisors were sent to Saudi Arabia in January 1955 to train Saudi military personnel housed in Taif.[42] (3) The Baghdad Pact rejection of 1955. In January 1955, Saudi Arabia, Egypt and Yemen jointly rejected the Baghdad Pact, a military defense pact sponsored by Western powers. In addition to rejecting the pact, President Nasser announced the need for joint Arab military action, which all three countries supported. (4) The Saudi Arabian-Egyptian-Syrian Tripartite Pact of 1955. Although its longevity was limited, a tripartite pact which focused on military and security matters was signed by Saudi Arabia, Egypt and Syria.[43] (5) The Jeddah Military Pact of 1956. This pact, signed personally by King Saud, Imam Ahmad and President Nasser in April 1956, strengthened and enforced the two mutual defense pacts of 1954.

The Jeddah agreement is significant for several reasons. First, it covered economic, military and political matters. It also demonstrated the parties' awareness of the rapidly changing nature of the economic, military and political situation in the Arab world, as well as the need for stronger and more constructive ties among themselves, particularly in the military arena. In fact, the pact went so far as to define armed aggression against any one of the parties to the pact as aggression against them all. In support of this stance, the parties committed themselves to aid the victim of the aggression through the use of any and all necessary means at their disposal, including the use of military force in order to repel the aggression and restore security and peace.[44]

Second, although the Jeddah Pact was only implemented once (during the French, British and Israeli tripartite attack on Egypt after the closure of the Suez Canal),[45] a number of writers have suggested that the pact was also used in 1962 by both Egypt and Saudi Arabia to justify their intervention in Yemen.[46] This suggestion, however, suffers from a fatal weakness concerning Saudi Arabia, namely, that Saudi Arabia never intervened militarily in Yemen. Its sole involvement took the form of moral and financial assistance, and even that was rendered only at the request of the deposed Imam. In contrast, President Nasser, who viewed the pact as a "collective security pact," did in fact use the Jeddah Military Pact to justify his military intervention in Yemen on the side of the rebels. King Saud, on the other hand, viewed it as a pact designed only to counter foreign military intervention.

In addition to the pacts outlined above, other examples of military cooperation among the three parties during the period between 1932 and 1962 abound. Among the more significant are: active joint partic-ipation in the Arab-Israeli War of 1948; Saudi Arabia's support of Imam

Yahya during the coup attempt of 1948 and its willingness to send military aid to him; and joint Saudi-Egyptian opposition to the ousting of Imam Ahmad in 1955. Although the arms Saudi Arabia sent the Imam's son, al-Badr, became unnecessary when the Imam succeeded in regaining his throne through his own efforts, it is important to note, first, that the arms were sent and, second, that the Egyptians, who opposed Abdallah because of his perceived Western sympathies, fully encouraged and supported the Saudi action.

As the preceding discussion makes clear, military relations among the three countries were particularly fruitful during the years under examination. The agreements, alignments and cooperation among the parties promoted a fuller understanding of the security issues jointly confronting them and helped them coordinate their efforts to deter perceived sources of danger and ward off threats to their independence. Further, as the first attempts to arrive at cooperative military positions among newly independent Arab states, they represent a significant achievement in modern Middle East history. Political and military relations among the three concerned parties during the period 1932–1962 present a picture of competing interests against a growing awareness of the interrelatedness of their concerns and developing political maturity. These relations took a dramatic turn with the coming of the 1962 coup in Yemen.

Notes

[1] H. C. Armstrong, *Lord of Arabia: A Biography of Abdul Aziz Ibn Saud* (Beirut: Khayats' College Book Cooperative), p. 184.

[2] Ahmad Assah, *Muajizatun fauq al-Rimal* [A Miracle on the Sands], 2nd ed. (Beirut: al-Matabi al-Ahliyah al-Lubnaniyah, 1966), p. 117. As a means of establishing its control over the Hejaz, the Saudi government in August 1926 promulgated a citizenship law which gave the right to Saudi citizenship to all Hejaz residents carrying Ottoman citizenship identification cards before World War I, or residing in the Hejaz continuously for three years, or born in the Hejaz. The government of King Fuad objected strenuously to the law, but the Saudi government countered these objections by explaining that the law was in the best interests of the Hejaz residents.

[3] Armstrong, pp. 184–187.

[4] Assah, p. 119. Other agreements, touching on post, customs, and navigation matters, were also reached at this time. Outstanding issues, such as the ones relating to the sending of the *kiswah* (the cover of the Kabah) and *mahmal* (a procession accompanying the yearly transfer of the *kiswah* to Saudi Arabia) were also settled. Amin Said, *Tarikh al-Dawlah al-Saudiyah* [History of the Saudi Dynasty], Vol. 2 (Beirut: Dar al-Katib al-Arabi, 1964), p. 232. Traditionally, Egypt sent the cover of *al-Kabah* to Saudi Arabia on a yearly basis. It was sent

by caravan from the port of Jeddah to Makkah, escorted by a band of musicians. This procession was called *al-mahmal.*

5 Said, pp. 170–192.

6 Assah, p. 121.

7 Though Imam Ahmad ruled Yemen from 1948 to 1962, he never raised the issue of the treaty which was to have expired in 1954. In the aftermath of the 1962 coup d'état in Yemen, the issue has been repeatedly raised and then dropped by successive republican regimes which have been preoccupied with internal problems. The present government in Sanaa is again demanding a review of the treaty, and both countries are now engaged in negotiations to reach a mutually satisfactory resolution of the issue. In a private interview with the author on October 9, 1984, a Saudi official involved in these negotiations said: "It is apparent that the current government in Sanaa does not want seriously to annex Najran and Jizan. What Sanaa wants exactly is to put pressure on Saudi Arabia so that it (Sanaa) can get more financial support and material aid from the kingdom.

8 Said, pp. 403–405.

9 David Holden and Richard Johns, *The House of Saud* (New York: Holt, Rinehart and Winston, 1981), p. 149.

10 Anwar al-Sadat, *In Search of Identity: An Autobiography* (New York: Harper Colophon Books, 1978), p. 61.

11 In his memoirs published in *al-Sharq al-Awsat* newspaper, Lt. General Mohammad Naguib stated that he was the one who set the timing for the coup d'état, or, as the Egyptians call it, the "1952 Revolution." Naguib also stated that Nasser, a colonel at that time, had suggested postponing the military move against the monarchy until August (1952), but that he (Naguib) insisted on July 23rd. See *al-Sharq al-Awsat* (October 17, 1984), p. 9. However, most other accounts give Nasser as the real power behind the coup.

12 The good relations enjoyed by Egypt and Saudi Arabia during this period are attested to by H.E. Mahmoud Riad, Egypt's foreign minister in 1964 and from 1967–1971. In an interview granted the author in Cairo on November 11, 1984, Mr. Riad stated that despite Saudi Arabia's neutrality, King Saud was called upon to mediate disputes between Nasser and Mohammad Naguib, demonstrating how close the two countries were. See Appendix No. 4, Question and Answer Number 1.

13 Robert Lacey, *The Kingdom: Arabia & the House of Sa'ud* (New York: Avon Books, 1981), p. 311.

14 Ibid.

15 Ibid., pp. 311–314.

16 Ibid., pp. 314–315.

17 Ibid.

18 Anthony H. Cordesman, *The Gulf and the Search for Strategic Stability: Saudi Arabia, the Military Balance in the Gulf, and Trends in the Arab-Israeli Military Balance* (Boulder, CO: Westview Press, 1984), p. 231.

19 Interview with a Saudi official.

20 Interview given to the author on November 11, 1984, in Cairo. See Appendix No. 4, Question and Answer Number 1.

[21] Interview with a Saudi official.

[22] Al-Sadat, p. 151.

[23] Author's translation.

[24] J. E. Peterson, *Yemen: The Search for a Modern State* (Baltimore: The Johns Hopkins University Press, 1982), p. 38.

[25] Prince Saud ibn Hazloul, *Tarikh Muluk al-Saud* [History of the Saudi Kings], 1st ed. (Riyadh: Riyadh Press, 1381/1960), pp. 226–229.

[26] The three would-be assassins were:

Name: Captain Ali Hizam al-Hadri
Occupation: Captain in the Yemeni Army
Passport No.: 98
Passport Date: Shawal 1, A.H. 1353 (A.D. 1935)
Place of Issue: Sanaa Passport Section

Name: Salih ibn Ali al-Hadriadri
Occupation: Farmer
Passport No.: 34
Passport Date: Shawal 1, A.H. 1353 (A.D. 1935)
Place of Issue: Sanaa Passport Section

Name: Musad ibn Ali ibn Hujayr
Occupation: Soldier in the Yemeni Army
Passport No.: 63
Passport Date: Dhu al-Qadah 5, A.H. 1353 (A.D. 1935)
Place of Issue: Issued by al-Sayyid Muhammad Faklan, Yemeni Emir of
    Pilgrimage

See also Prince Hazloul, p. 228, for more details.

[27] The pact was effective for ten years and was to be considered automatically renewed if none of the signatories filed for termination one year before its expiration date. See also Said, pp. 257–265.

[28] Abdallah al-Wazir negotiated and signed the 1934 Saudi-Yemeni agreement on behalf of Imam Yahya in al-Taif. It should be noted that the al-Taif of this treaty was a small fishing village in Yemen and not the Saudi Arabian city. See also Dr. Ribhi Tahir Sahwil, "Al-Harakah al-Wataniyah wa Atharuha alal-Harakat 1962 fil-Jumhuriyya al-Arabiya al-Yamaniyah" [The National Movement and Its Impact on the 1962 Movement in the Yemen Arab Republic], in *Thawrat 26 Sibtambir: Dirasat wa Shahadat lil-Tarikh* [September 26 Revolution: Studies and Evidence for History], 1st ed. 1981–82 (Beirut: Maktabat al-Jumahir, for Yemeni Center for Analysis and Studies, Sanaa), pp. 37–41.

[29] Assah, p. 125.

[30] George Lenczowski, *The Middle East in World Affairs*, 4th ed. (Ithaca: Cornell University Press, 1980), pp. 612–622.

[31] Cordesman, p. 457.

[32] Manfred W. Wenner, *Modern Yemen: 1918–1966* (Baltimore: The Johns Hopkins Press, 1967), pp. 114–117.

³³ After succeeding in overcoming his captors, Imam Ahmad went outside his palace, took his sword and told the rebels that he was their ruler and anyone who objected to his leadership should take out his sword and fight him personally. No one challenged him and he regained his throne.

³⁴ Mohammed Ahmad Zabarah, *Yemen: Tradition vs. Modernity* (New York: Praeger, 1982), p. 56.

³⁵ Lenczowski, p. 623.

³⁶ Interview with a ranking Saudi official.

³⁷ Abdallah ibn Ali ibn Misfir, *Akhbar Asir* [News of Asir] (Damascus: al-Maktab al-Islami, 1978), pp. 191–197.

³⁸ The city of Taif is the summer capital of Saudi Arabia. The talks were conducted in an area called "Bayn al-Shajaratain" ("between the two trees"), now known as the al-Khalidiah district.

³⁹ Sayid Mustafa Salim, *Takwin al-Yaman al-Hadith: al-Yaman wal-Imam Yahya (1904–1948)* [The Structure of Modern Yemen: Yemen and Imam Yahya (1904–1948)], 3rd ed. (Cairo: Maktabat Medbouli, 1984), p. 544.

⁴⁰ Ibid., pp. 544–548.

⁴¹ Said, p. 263.

⁴² Muhammad Sadiq Aql and Hiyam Abu Afiyah, *Adwa ala Thawrat al-Yaman* [Lights on the Yemen Revolution] (Cairo: Dar al-Qawmiyah lil-Tibaah wal-Nashr), p. 68.

⁴³ Lacey, p. 311.

⁴⁴ During the author's interview with H.E. Mahmoud Riad on November 11, 1984, he attributed the failure of the pact to the insistence of Khalid al-Azm, Syria's then–prime minister, on having an immediate and complete union among the three countries, including total economic unity. In contrast, Egypt was solely concerned with security matters.

⁴⁵ Saudi Arabia offered Egypt use of its airfields in 1956. Ghazi Abdulrahman Algosaibi, "The 1962 Revolution in Yemen and Its Impact on the Foreign Policies of the U.A.S. and Saudi Arabia," Ph.D. dissertation, University College, University of London, 1970, p. 171.

⁴⁶ Mohammed Khalil, ed., *The Arab States and the Arab League*, vol. II, article no. 2 (Beirut: Khayats, 1962), p. 251. Also see Arabic text of the Pact, Annex No. (6) taken from *al-Wathaiq al-Arabiyah* [Arab Political Documents] (Beirut: American University of Beirut, 1967), pp. 45–52.

Chapter 3

THE COUP D'ETAT AND THE EGYPTIAN INTERVENTION IN NORTH YEMEN IN 1962

The anti-monarchial coup d'état in North Yemen was the result of several factors. Throughout its reign over North Yemen as an independent kingdom (1918–1962), the Hamid al-Din family encountered crucial circumstances internally, as well as criticism externally. However, the *Mutawakilite* system survived all the pre-1962 coup attempts and the Hamid al-Din family continued their rule of the country until September 26, 1962. But the 1962 coup d'état differed quite markedly from the preceding ones. In 1962 an external military force, i.e., the Egyptian troops, dictated the rules of the game and succeeded in ousting the Imam and his family from Yemen. In fact, Egypt actually planned and helped to execute the military takeover in 1962 in Yemen.[1]

Factors Leading to the Coup

The 1962 coup d'état in Yemen can be attributed to a multiplicity of factors which can most easily be classified as internal and external.

Internal Factors: Backwardness, Isolation, Opposition

The name al-Yaman probably derives from the Arabic word for "happiness" or "prosperity" and accords with the Roman designation "Arabia Felix."[2] Despite its name, Yemen until the end of the 1950s was among the most backward countries in the world. Until 1918 much of Yemen was under the control of the Ottoman Empire. The Imams, Yemen's traditional rulers, were recognized by the Turks as the spiritual heads of the Zaydi subsect of Shii and also served as temporal rulers in areas not under Ottoman domination. After the Turks departed Yemen following World War I, the Hamid al-Din family of Imams maintained their control over the country by keeping and extending their powers through any available means. Under the Imams, Yemen's backwardness, isolation and the strength of its opposition forces, were the most critical internal factors leading to the 1962 coup.

Traditionally, Yemen was highly fragmented in social terms and social mobility was almost unknown. Society and politics were dominated by the *Sayyids*, descendants of the Prophet Muhammad, whose position as the upper elite of the country was unchallengeable. For a thousand years every Zaydi Imam came from one of the aristocratic *Sayyid* families. The *qadis*, subordinate to the *Sayyids*, provided the middle-ranking civil servants of the country. Although the rank of *qadi* was not necessarily hereditary, a number of old *qadi* families had become prominent over the centuries.[3] The great majority of the Yemenis, however, were tribesmen, who could not aspire to *Sayyid* status and rarely became *qadis*. Their resentment, especially in Shafii tribes, of *Sayyid* power and wealth contributed to the attempts against the Imams in 1948 and 1962. Furthermore, each tribe was largely independent of the state and often engaged in bitter struggle with rival tribes, which served to deepen the divisions between Yemenis.

The existence of strong tribal loyalties further contributed to Yemen's backwardness and represented a major problem for the central government. Though the government has attempted to lessen the divisive effects of conflicting loyalties, tribalism still exists today and is likely to remain a major divisive force in Yemen, representing a major challenge to the authority of any central government.[4]

Education, or lack of it, was another prominent factor in Yemen's backwardness. Throughout the Imamate rule in Yemen, the Imams paid little attention to education. Only primary instruction in religious matters in schools known as *kuttab* existed in cities and towns. Even these classes, which were affiliated with the mosques and which taught students the Quran and how to read and write, were not financially supported by the government but rather were maintained from income received from *awqaf* (Islamic endowments).[5]

Few economic opportunities existed for Yemenis, fostering a sense of economic insecurity among the populace. Accusations that the ruling family expanded its wealth by purchasing lands from the citizens at cheap prices and by controlling the import-export markets further contributed to the country's economic woes and the general malaise.[6]

Agriculture largely was neglected throughout the Imamate rule, despite its being the predominant source of income in Yemen. Of 5.5 million acres suitable for cultivation in Yemen, only five percent was cultivated by the private sector. Modern equipment and new techniques of cultivation were not introduced, and Yemeni farmers continued to labor using their grandfathers' tools. These conditions obviously inhibited the economic development of the country. As in the case of agriculture, the Imams did not attempt to introduce new industrial methods into the country. Even worse, the making of textiles using the old methods ceased when in 1956 the government started exporting locally grown cotton and replacing it with imported, ready-made clothes.[7] Other local industries such as the handicrafts of making robes and leather goods suffered similarly due to the industrial policies of the Imams.

Trade, because it was neglected, also suffered under the Imams. They formulated no rules or regulations to govern or promote foreign commerce and undertook no steps to create a Yemeni currency. Further, in order to flourish, trade requires good means of transportation. Here, too, the Imams proved inadequate. They took no steps to obtain modern vehicles, to develop good roads, or to devise good maps of the country. In total, these oversights resulted in a virtual absence of foreign commerce. Even the then-existing seaports and airports were not supplied with their basic requirements.

In order to insure the loyalty of those tribes they had conquered, both Imam Yahya and Imam Ahmad, when confronted with a tribe which refused to recognize their authority, resorted to the practice of taking hostages in order to force the tribe into submission. Usually, the hostage was either a son or a brother of a chief of the tribe or a prominent leader of it.[8] This practice may have generated hatred and resentment while costing the Imam a good deal of prestige. This is true despite the fact that, through it, the Imam was able to control his enemies and force them to accept his authority.

As a result of these practices and attitudes, Yemen, in the first half of the twentieth century, remained one of the most backward countries in the world. Its position prompted King Abd al-Aziz to advise Imam Ahmad in the aftermath of the unsuccessful 1948 coup to begin modernizing Yemen by creating modern government institutions, building schools, and developing the most needed infrastructure of the country.[9] The advice, however, largely went unheeded.

Certainly, one of the most critical blunders Imam Yahya made during the three decades he ruled Yemen (1918–1948) was his unyielding belief that he could safeguard the country from outside threats and thereby maintain its independence. By severely limiting his contacts with other countries, by eschewing involvement in international and regional political affairs, and by refusing to allow foreigners into his country (including foreign diplomats), the Imam made Yemen a strange and backward country in the eyes of the world. This perception eventually precipitated the very interference he had sought to avoid. His isolationism and xenophobia are clearly evidenced in the fact that, although he joined both the Arab League in 1945 and the United Nations in 1947, he nevertheless permitted no foreign diplomats to reside in Yemen.[10] At the time of his assassination in 1948, Imam Yahya had sent only one ambassador abroad, to Cairo.

His successor, Imam Ahmad, tried to deviate from his father's isolationist policy in several ways. He established diplomatic relations with Arab and non-Arab countries, and in a similar fashion, entered into a number of treaties and pacts with various states. In a further attempt to bring Yemen out of its isolation, on March 8, 1958, Yemen joined the newly proclaimed United Arab States with Egypt and Syria.

All Imam Ahmad's efforts to introduce Yemen to the modern era were unsuccessful, however, as he did little to reform the internal structure of the country. Yemen remained governed by an absolute ruler, there were no modern governmental institutions and the country as a whole had not undergone any modernization. The lack of progress on the domestic front in turn generated support for Yemen's already existing opposition force. Eventually, the country's dissatisfaction with the lethargic pace of modernization manifested itself in the unsuccessful attempt in 1955 to remove Imam Ahmad from power. As H.E. Mahmoud Riad commented in a private interview with the author in 1984:

I repeat that the Egyptian intervention in Yemen moved it, in a brief period of time, from the Dark Ages into the twentieth century. Those who saw Yemen in 1962 and then saw it again in 1974 can see the difference between the two periods.[11]

The third internal factor, the opposition forces, might well be considered the most important, and it grew out of the preceding two, backwardness and isolation. In Yemen, the opposition comprised four groups: educated Yemenis who had been schooled in Iraq, Aden, Egypt and other Arab countries in the 1930s, 1940s and 1950s; aristocratic families such as the al-Wazir; oppressed tribesmen; and military intellectuals. In 1936 the first secret opposition group, composed primarily of high school and university graduates, was formed with three branches in Sanaa, Taiz and *Ibn al-Hajriah*. This was followed in 1940 by the formation of another organization, the Shabab al-Amr bil-Maruf, or The Youth of Peaceful Order. These two organizations were crushed by the Yemeni authorities in 1943, forcing many of their members, mostly intellectuals and aristocrats, to flee to Aden (South Yemen), where they established the Free Yemeni Party.[12]

In 1948, Abdallah al-Wazir, a prominent member of an aristocratic family, seized the throne following the assassination of Imam Yahya.

He ruled for only 26 days before Imam Ahmad succeeded in overthrowing him. This incident was followed in 1952 by the formation of the Yemeni Union. The Union had among its supporters prominent members of the press, such as Abdallah bin Ali al-Hakami and Abdallah Abd al-Wahab Numan, of the newspapers *al-Salam* and *al-Fusul*. The Union's avowed purpose was to direct and organize a mass movement, as well as to supervise the activities of the press. These internal and external opposition activities culminated in the ill-fated, family-oriented coup of 1955, which suffered the same fate as the unsuccessful 1948 coup. Undeterred, the plotters tried again in March 1961, when another failed assassination attempt against Imam Ahmad was made, this time while he was receiving medical treatment at al-Hudaydah hospital.[13]

The military opposition in Yemen began in the late 1940s in Cairo and received the full encouragement of the Egyptians, particularly after the 1952 Egyptian revolution. In 1948, fourteen Yemeni officers joined the Egyptian War College. Soon after, they were exposed to revolutionary slogans and Egyptian propaganda. Within a short while these Yemeni cadets began to reformulate their political views similar to those held by their Egyptian instructors. However, this group and others, including the tribes, never organized themselves or established their own anti-monarchial movement. Their activities were limited to discussions held during social gatherings and during the *"qat" majlis*. The so-called "Liberal Officers' Movement" consisted only of junior officers whose influence was limited and whose activities were disorganized.

External Factors: Yemenis Abroad, Egyptian Influence, Soviet Influence

In treating this aspect of the causes and factors leading up to the 1962 coup, it is important to remember that the modern world evolved into an interdependent one. The Yemeni Imams, however, mistakenly believed that by insulating Yemen from the outside world they could live peacefully in splendid isolation, dependent only upon themselves and Yemen's natural resources. Nevertheless, despite this intent, by the mid-1940s Imam Yahya found himself bound by a number of international and regional treaties. Hence, by definition, he became drawn into increasing contact with, and aimless growing commitments to, foreign governments. His son and successor, Imam Ahmad, continued this trend with his more open foreign policy, thereby committing himself, with the support and encouragement of Crown Prince Muhammad al-Badr, to more and more external contacts. This policy, in turn, had far-reaching effects.

The dearth of jobs and educational opportunities in Yemen forced many Yemeni citizens to immigrate both to Arab and non-Arab countries.

In 1961, the number of Yemenis living outside Yemen—in other Arab states, Ethiopia, Somalia, France, England and the United States—was estimated by one source at approximately 600,000.[14] At the same time, the Yemeni government sent many civilian and military students abroad to undergo specific job training, to receive higher education or to attend a military academy. All this was accomplished in accordance with bilateral treaties signed by Yemen and those Arab and non-Arab states. Since Yemenis' ties to each other and to their homeland are so strong, married men in particular often left their wives behind and regularly sent considerable amounts of money (remittances) home to them. This practice meant that a sizeable amount of foreign currency circulated inside Yemen, providing a beneficial side effect.

On the other hand, these returning immigrants and students brought with them new ideas and political thoughts into Yemen, and these, too, left their imprint on Yemeni society. While living in modern, open societies such as the United States, England and France, Yemenis became exposed to the ideas of freedom, democracy, equality and justice. Military students, in turn, learned the meaning of revolution, the full import of the power they wielded, and the salient role they could play in transforming their backward country into a modern revolutionary state. One such military official wrote:

> We have grown up and our rational responsibility has grown up too. When the July 23, 1952, revolution in Egypt materialized, the hope in the salvation of our country from the backward and dirty rule increased. We the youth of our country are the hope for our nation, and by our hand salvation will occur. . . .[15]

With the same aspirations and the same line of political thinking, other Yemeni groups residing or studying abroad engaged in unorganized and semi-organized activities aimed at discrediting the Imamate rule in Yemen. They operated from Aden, Cairo and Beirut, among other capitals, and shared a common goal: to bring down the Hamid al-Din family in Yemen.

Undoubtedly, the extent of Egyptian influence on Yemeni students and military cadets, both inside Yemen and in Cairo, was great and intensive. Both the 1955 military tripartite pact among Egypt, Yemen and Saudi Arabia, and the 1958 union among Egypt, Yemen and Syria, eased the way for the spread of Egyptian influence and ideas among Yemeni youth and military cadets, in addition to offering Egypt a way to infiltrate Yemen as a whole. By 1959, Egyptian military personnel, teachers, doctors, and office managers were to be found throughout Yemen. Moreover, by 1961 there were 300–400 Yemenis in Egyptian secondary schools and more than 100 Yemeni students enrolled at Cairo University. By that same year, 1961, even Egyptian intelligence officers were operating actively in Sanaa. When the author asked ex-Imam al-Badr about the role of the Egyptian embassy in Yemen in 1961, he replied:

> There was an Egyptian diplomat called Mohammed Abd al-Wahed working at the Egyptian embassy in Sanaa. He had more authority than the ambassador, Ahmad Abu Zayd. In fact, this Abd al-Wahed was the representative of Egyptian Intelligence in Yemen, and used to encourage the Yemenis to carry out demonstrations and conduct some acts of violence against the rule of my father, the late Imam Ahmad, who used to tell him frankly, "I don't like you, I always suspect you, and I suspect your behavior and your motives."[16]

The foregoing observations help to explain how Egyptian influence, as an external factor in the causes behind the 1962 coup, was decisive. Moreover, the second major external factor in the coup is directly attributable to Egyptian influence, namely, the Russian infiltration of Yemen. Despite the November 1, 1928, ten-year bilateral treaty of friendship and commerce between Yemen and the Soviet Union, Soviet influence was absent in Yemen before the mid-1950s. The sole results of that initial treaty had consisted of Soviet diplomatic representation in Sanaa and the presence of some doctors and a trade delegation at al-Hudaydah.[17] Inconsequently, the first article of the treaty recognized the complete independence of Yemen and of its Imam.

Although the diplomatic mission and the trade delegation had tried to undercut Western influence in Yemen, it met with little success. This was true despite the fact that the Soviet consular representatives were Muslims, which made it easy for them to engage in direct contact with the Yemeni people.[18] As a result, though the treaty was renewed in 1938 for another ten years, Soviet impatience led them to recall the entire mission later that same year, an act they subsequently regretted, particularly after the outbreak of World War II. Eager to become a maritime power, and wishing to assume the role formerly occupied by Germany and Italy after their defeat in that war, the Soviets renewed their approaches to the Imam of Yemen. These approaches ultimately led to the Imam's acceptance of Soviet technicians who were scheduled to arrive in Yemen before the end of 1946.[19] The reestablishment of diplomatic relations formally took place in 1955.

The most significant Soviet role in Yemen began in 1956 with the visit of Crown Prince Muhammad al-Badr to Cairo. With Nasser's full support and encouragement, the crown prince continued on to Moscow, where he signed a treaty of friendship and mutual aid with the Soviets.

In 1957, after running into serious disagreements with the British over Aden, Crown Prince al-Badr made his ties to the Soviets even more explicit, saying that times had changed, that "1957 was not like 1954," and that the Imam now had "the greatest power on earth behind him, Russia."[20] Soviet experts and military advisers were brought in, and Russian equipment and weapons began arriving for Yemen's armed forces. A sign of the growing confidence of the Soviets is to be found in the example of one of their officers, a man who was a close associate of the Soviet ambassador in Sanaa, and who began to incite army personnel against the tribal shaykhs.[21] Further, by 1961 about 300 Yemenis were being trained in Communist-bloc countries, particularly the Soviet Union.[22] Yemen's turn to the Soviet Union may be attributed to its perception of the West in terms of Great Britain's colonial policies and the British-American sponsored Baghdad Pact, which was regarded as anti-Yemeni. Therefore, the participation in the Jeddah Pact of 1956, the joining of the United Arab States in 1958, and the turn towards the Soviet Union and Eastern-bloc countries were felt to be demonstrations of independence.[23] In addition, Yemen could afford to send students abroad only if they were provided scholarships, and the Soviet Union was the only state to provide them.

All in all, one may conclude that Soviet activities within Yemen were aimed at politically influencing Yemenis and encouraging Yemeni youth to adopt Soviet ideological slogans. Those Yemeni youth who received their education and military training in the Soviet Union were the most impressionable group. They returned to Yemen with new ideas that were nothing less than revolutionary in a country such as Yemen.

External factors leading to the 1962 coup in Yemen contributed substantially to discrediting the royal family. Yemenis who immigrated and who were educated abroad were exposed to new ideas and influenced by them. Their changed expectations of government—in great part a result of Soviet and Egyptian campus influence—led to their dissatisfaction with the ruling elite. When these Yemenis returned to their homeland, their views in turn influenced those who remained at home. Among these factors, the Egyptian influence was the most significant and deliberate, as will be shown in the next section.

The Coup, Egyptian Involvement and the International Legal Aspects of the Intervention

The Coup and Egyptian Involvement

Although many changes which might well be described as revolutionary took place in Yemeni politics and society after the overthrow of the Imam, his ouster on September 26, 1962, was in fact a coup d'état.

Nonetheless, Yemenis, like many other Arab states which have had a regime overthrown (e.g., Iraq, Syria, Egypt and Libya), prefer to call it a revolution. Imam Muhammad al-Badr succeeded his father, Imam Ahmad, on September 19, 1962. Eight days later, at about midnight, a small armored column of six T-34 tanks and four armored vehicles arrived in Sanaa, the capital, from the seaport city of al-Hudaydah. This was the beginning of the coup.

According to the description of events given by Imam al-Badr during a 1983 interview, an attempt to assassinate him took place before the bombardment of the palace started, that is, at approximately 11:30 p.m. At that time, Husayn al-Sukari, a junior army officer and deputy chief in charge of security for the royal palace, tried to assassinate him as he walked toward the residential part of the palace, following a meeting of the new Council of Ministers.[24] The assassination attempt failed when the rifle's trigger jammed, and the assassin was captured by the Imam's personal guards after shooting himself in the chin. A few minutes later, while the Imam rested in his palace, the electricity was cut off and the sounds of an armored column entering the area surrounding the royal palace could be heard. At 11:30 p.m., the tanks opened fire on the palace; simultaneously, rebel troops of the Yemeni army seized the Sanaa radio station and the airfield. The Imam, after resisting for about 24 hours, survived and escaped to the northern part of the country. Once there, he began gathering followers among the tribes in an effort to oppose the new regime in Sanaa.

Contrary to what has been said about the leader of the coup d'état being Colonel Abdallah al-Sallal, who had been appointed by the Imam himself as Commander of the "Royal Guard," the ringleader of the coup and the principal Yemeni planner of it, according to the Imam, was an officer called Abd al-Ghani. Also according to the Imam, it is possible that Abd al-Ghani, who was killed during the early hours of the coup, was the one who had been in constant contact with the Egyptian embassy in Sanaa.[25]

The coup d'état of 1962 apparently was engineered and pre-arranged by President Nasser of Egypt. Cairo itself behaved before and after the coup in a way that indicates it was behind the move and perhaps even planned it. The following points contribute to and support this conclusion:

1. President Nasser took advantage of Yemen's and Egypt's entrance into a confederation in February 1958 to begin indoctrinating Yemeni military students studying in Egypt as part of the mutual agreements between the two countries.

2. In the fall of 1959, Nasser began choosing the men to be appointed as his instruments in this plot to overthrow the monarchy in Yemen and replace it with a republican system.

3. In December 1961, a call for revolution in North Yemen was broadcast by Cairo Radio.

4. On January 4 and 5, 1962, Cairo Radio announced that Egypt was trying to reconcile nationalist aims for the liberation of Yemen, Aden and the Aden protectorates.

5. Anti-monarchy Yemenis were broadcasting from the "Voice of the Arabs" radio station in Cairo.

6. On September 19, 1962, the day Imam Ahmad died, the "Voice of the Arabs" in Cairo spoke of the coming revolution in Yemen, in which the people's "true feelings to the Imam" would be made known.[26]

The coup d'état took place only eight days after the "Voice of the Arabs" broadcast announcing the coming revolution. In addition, Imam al-Badr confirmed the early Egyptian involvement by saying:

> Abd al-Nasser was working to achieve this goal [the overthrow of the Imamate in Yemen]. However, he started moving in this direction in 1960, particularly after my rejection of his offer to cooperate with him in overthrowing the Saudi regime as a step towards controlling the Arabian Peninsula. Nevertheless, the brainwashing of the Yemenis, the military as well as the youth, had been carried out by the Islamic Center in Cairo, then headed by Anwar al-Sadat. Secret contacts with Yemenis were conducted by this Center inside and outside Yemen under many Islamic slogans. In the meantime, Abd al-Rahman al-Baidani, who is originally an Egyptian and married to al-Sadat's wife's sister, had played a vital role in this direction, too, i.e., brainwashing of the Yemenis.[27]

The Imam also acknowledged the role of the Egyptian Embassy in Sanaa in cooperating with the rebels and planning the coup.[28]

Finally, the Egyptian involvement in the coup was confirmed immediately after the rebels began bombarding the royal palace. The Egyptian military mission in Sanaa had secretly helped to put some of the Soviet armored vehicles into running order.[29] At the same time, the Imam himself confirmed that in the early morning following the coup, and during the time of his 24-hour counterattack against the rebels, he and his supporters saw helicopters landing near the palace and in the vicinity of Sanaa airport. He interpreted this to mean that either these helicopters were on board ships anchored near the Yemeni coast, or they were assembled inside the Egyptian embassy in Sanaa.[30]

The Egyptian adventure did not end with the coup but continued even after the early October reappearance of the legitimate ruler of Yemen, Imam Muhammad al-Badr, in Yemen's north and his announcement that he would fight to regain his throne. On October 1, 1962, Nasser sent paratroopers and military equipment to Yemen, and

Egyptian ships began landing at al-Hudaydah shipyard carrying tanks, arms, ammunition and staff officers.[31] This is disputed by H.E. Mahmoud Riad, who, when interviewed by the author, referred to a book entitled *The Story of the July 23 Revolution: Abd al-Nasser and the Arabs*, by Ahmed Hamrush. Mr. Hamrush explained that the Egyptian intervention in Yemen started with only two airplanes and about 300 Egyptian soldiers.[32] If Mr. Hamrush's facts are accurate, they indicate that Nasser greatly miscalculated the price of his intervention in Yemen, thereby recklessly involving Egypt in a very costly war.

There are those Nasserists who try to defend Nasser's position by claiming that Egypt's intervention in Yemen was the prime responsibility of Anwar al-Sadat.[33] Al-Sadat himself acknowledged that he was the first to support the "Yemeni Revolution" and that he was the one who convinced the "Presidential Council of Egypt" of the necessity of supporting it as well.[34]

International Law and the Decision to Intervene

The traditional principle of nonintervention as developed by the nations of the West[35] has been qualified by a number of exceptions. There is a rough consensus that these exceptions include the following: intervention by invitation of an incumbent government, or counterintervention, possibly, by invitation of insurgents; intervention to protect the lives and property of a state's own nationals and other aliens from clear and present danger; humanitarian intervention to protect the indigenous population of a state or some minority thereof from violations of its human rights; and intervention by treaty right.[36]

On the basis of these aspects of international law, we will now examine the legal and moral implications of the Egyptian intervention in North Yemen. The question of why President Nasser of Egypt decided to intervene in North Yemen was insightfully addressed by Robert W. Stookey:

President Nasser's persistent effort to exert discipline over foreign policies of all Arab states in Egypt's own interest, had failed dismally. He had publicly undertaken to destroy the surviving Arab monarchies. Syria had renounced union with Egypt and joined Iraq in repudiating Cairo's lead of the Arab left wing. Nasser was on polite terms within the Arab world, with only the new nation of Algeria. He sorely needed some external success to restore his damaged prestige. Yemen appeared to offer an opportunity to reassert leadership, strike a blow at monarchy and reaction; and mold a new Yemeni society in the Egyptian image, all at negligible effort or cost.[37]

The same conclusion is supported by Mahmoud Riad, who confirms that when the Yemen revolution took place in 1962 Egypt was in a state of shock and frustration as a result of the deterioration in Egyptian-Arab relations and the collapse of the federation with Syria.[38]

Thus, it appears that President Nasser's decision to intervene in Yemen was more a product of ill-conceived hopes of reestablishing Egypt as the leader of the Arab left than of an appreciation for the realities of his Yemeni policies. Moreover, it also appears that Nasser's miscalculation in Yemen was reinforced by hopes for personal political gain. For five years (1962–1967), he was to pay for this miscalculation in huge economic costs, which otherwise could have been spent on Egyptian development, and in political costs, in terms of his prestige in the Arab world. In addition, the Egyptian intervention in Yemen undoubtedly damaged the Egyptian army and contributed to the weakening of its morale. Throughout the five years of bitter fighting in Yemen, the Egyptian army lost approximately 26,000 of its best officers and enlisted men.[39]

There is a fine line to be drawn between vital support and total control. The 1962 coup was controlled by Egypt, and it certainly would have failed—and in fact might not even have been attempted—without Egyptian support. Moreover, since Egyptian military assistance for the new republican regime in Yemen was already en route before the coup, and since Egyptian military mission personnel actually assisted rebel troops by secretly redeploying Soviet-made military vehicles for the attempt, one can logically conclude that Nasser intervened in the domestic affairs of Yemen contrary to the accepted principles of international law. Egyptian vessels loaded with paratroopers and military equipment began landing at the port of al-Hudaydah on October 1, 1962, just five days after the coup.[40] In order for them to have arrived by then, they would have to have embarked from Egypt *before* the coup, clearly suggesting Nasser's foreknowledge and predetermined intent to intervene.

On November 10, 1962, a treaty of mutual defense was established between Egypt and North Yemen. This treaty subsequently obliged Nasser to increase the number of his troops in Yemen; this number reached 40,000 fully equipped men by 1964. This increase in troops was made necessary by the strong resistance of the royalists, that is, the supporters of the ex-Imam. In the meantime, this unexpected resistance ultimately began to undermine the morale of the Egyptian troops, and in April 1964 President Nasser himself visited Yemen to shore up the failing morale of his troops.[41] By that time, however, it had become obvious that a stalemate had set in and a civil war was in progress. The Egyptians could, for the most part, hold the main cities and towns, but they could not defeat the royalists.

International Law and the Conduct of War

In addition to Egypt's original decision to intervene, its conduct during the course of the Yemen Civil War can also be scrutinized in terms of international law. For example, the Geneva Convention of 1949, acknowledging that war is inevitable, took a pragmatic approach to it and produced standards of war conduct. In 1969, the United Nations, along with the International Committee of the Red Cross (ICRC), reaffirmed and clarified those aspects of international law regulating armed conflict in order to provide greater guarantees for protected persons, particularly civilians.[42] In the same year, the United Nations General Assembly unanimously adopted Resolution Number 2444, which recognized the following specific principles: that the right of the parties to a conflict to adopt means of injuring the enemy is not unlimited; that it is prohibited to launch attacks against the civilian population as such; that distinction must be made at all times between persons taking part in the hostilities and members of the civilian population to the effect that the civilian be spared as much as possible.[43]

Subsequent General Assemblies have adopted numerous resolutions, such as General Assembly Resolution Number 2675 (24th Session), entitled "Resolution on Protection of Civilians." These subsequent classifications serve to underscore the original intent of the Geneva Protocol of 1925. This Protocol is the first and most important document regulating the conduct of war applicable to Egypt's conduct as a combatant in the Yemeni Civil War: it prohibited military use of asphyxiating, poisonous or other gases, and of bacteriological methods of warfare.[44]

As Egypt became a full-fledged combatant, its methods of fighting increasingly conflicted with international law regarding the acceptable means of conducting a war. For example, in seeking to protect the new republican regime in Yemen, Egypt allegedly set out to exterminate the remaining members of the royal family. One of its means for accomplishing this was to set up bounties: a reward of 1,500 pounds was offered for a royal family member killed or captured.[45] In the meantime, the Egyptians indiscriminately bombed pro-royalists inside Yemen, destroying villages far from the main fighting, killing hundreds of civilians and causing thousands of others to live under trees or in caves with little food and with crops untended.[46] The Egyptians also used napalm bombs to destroy the crops of royalist tribes in order to starve them into submission. Inflicting civilian casualties as a deliberate strategy is clearly contrary to the Geneva Convention and the related Protocol.

International Law Violations Beyond North Yemen's Borders

In addition to the violations discussed above, Egyptian forces in Yemen proper broadened the war beyond Yemen's boundaries by attacking and occupying territory in South Yemen (then the Aden Protectorate) and conducting air strikes against the Saudi border towns of Najran and Jizan.[47]

By attacking and occupying territories in South Yemen, President Nasser of Egypt added a new dimension to the Egyptian intervention and role in Yemen. During his visit to Sanaa in April 1964, Nasser announced an increase in Egyptian assistance to the revolutionaries in South Yemen in order to oust the British from Aden. This assistance included support for dissident and terrorist groups and such activities as dropping explosive cigarettes inside the South Yemeni territories.[48] Despite the fact that the Egyptian tactics may have helped South Yemen to gain its independence in 1967, such activities, viewed from the standpoint of international law, were nevertheless immoral and unjustified.

Nasser's bombardment of Saudi Arabia began in November 1962, almost six months before Saudi Arabia decided to help the ousted Imam and his followers.[49] Richard Beeston of *The Times* (London) arrived in the Jizan area only three hours after it was bombed in May 1964. He described the situation as follows: "The whole population of some 30,000 people had fled to the beaches, and water supplies had been cut off . . . on the islands."[50]

In addition, as a result of a previous attack on Abha in the spring of 1963, 36 patients inside an Abha hospital were killed.[51] It is difficult to discern any military purpose served by attacks on the civilian population of Jizan, Abha and Najran, and they therefore appear to be contrary to international rules concerning the conduct of war. Nasser's real motives appear to have been to create a state of unrest within Saudi Arabia, forcing the kingdom to stop its aid to the royalists and possibly even to overthrow the regime.

When his tactic of attacking Saudi Arabia fell short of its goals, Nasser turned to subversion. Egypt trained and infiltrated Yemeni saboteurs into Saudi Arabia. Toward the end of 1966, those Egyptian-backed saboteurs succeeded in detonating a number of bombs inside the kingdom, including three in Riyadh, the capital, and one near Dammam in the Eastern Province. In early 1967, another group of saboteurs was sent into the kingdom in an attempt to assassinate the king. Charged with planting bombs under a bridge over which the king was scheduled to pass, the saboteurs failed, were captured and confessed to planning and carrying out acts of sabotage.[52]

During the *hajj* period of 1966, the Egyptian embassy in Jeddah tried to take advantage of the occasion by planting a number of bombs within the *hajj* ceremonial areas. Saudi security authorities discovered the attempt and the late King Faisal himself authorized one of his political advisers to warn the Egyptian ambassador that if the bombs were deployed strong Saudi retaliatory action would be taken against Egypt.[53]

Conclusions

There is little doubt that the 1962 coup d'état was caused both by internal factors—especially Yemen's backwardness, isolation, and opposition forces—as well as external factors—particularly Yemenis abroad, Egyptian influence both in and outside Yemen and Soviet influence also in and outside Yemen. In the meantime, the assassination of Imam Yahya in 1948 and the brief takeover of the government after his death, the 1955 attempted coup d'état, and the assassination attempt against Imam Ahmad's life in 1961 all indicate how Yemenis themselves were dissatisfied with the Imamate system. Nevertheless, the succession of Imam Muhammad al-Badr in 1962, who was known as an open-minded person, was looked upon by the Yemeni people and many other Arab and non-Arab states as a promising step towards modernizing the country and putting an end to its isolation. However, the new Imam was not able to achieve anything; he was overthrown after only eight days of his reign.

On the other hand, the Egyptian military intervention in Yemen appears largely responsible for the outbreak of the Yemeni Civil War. In fact, this intervention was a miscalculation on the part of President Nasser of Egypt, who anticipated an easy victory in Yemen. Faced with strong resistance from the ex-Imam and his supporters, Nasser was obliged to increase the number of his troops day by day. In the meantime, Nasser's determination to win that "unwinnable" war, at any cost and regardless of humanitarian aspects, led him to violate international rules and regulations covering war conduct. For example, in 1964, he sent Field Marshal Abd al-Hakim Amir to Yemen in an attempt to pacify the tribes supporting the ex-Imam (royalists). For about three months, Amir personally supervised a series of operations which later became known as the "Ramadan Offensive" because it coincided with the Muslim fasting month of Ramadan. The Ramadan Offensive was only partially successful, bringing about half of the country under Republican control.[54]

In the face of 80,000 troops, tanks and aircraft, the poorly equipped and trained royalists turned to guerilla tactics. Knowing the terrain well, they were able to elude the Egyptians, whom they harassed constantly by mining major roads and conducting hit-and-run raids on isolated outposts.[55] It was a situation not unlike Afghanistan today; accordingly, the Egyptians, like the Soviets in Afghanistan, tried to counter with a scorched-earth policy—ultimately including the use of poison gas, a substance which is outlawed because of its indiscriminate fatal effect on all living things. Furthermore, this control effectively took place from 1964 to 1966, when "Nasser reduced the Yemen republic from the status of a partner to that of a servant, dominated by an army of occupation."[56] President Nasser and his men in Yemen were the real rulers of the country in the aftermath of the 1962 coup d'état. As a matter of fact, at one point Nasser had imprisoned the entire Yemeni government in Cairo.[57]

Beyond question, the situation in Yemen had posed serious problems for Nasser. His decision to attack Saudi borders meant that for the first time in ten years as Egypt's president he would initiate offensive military action against an Arab state. He justified his break with tradition on the grounds that he was helping the progressive forces in Yemen.[58] Nevertheless, Egypt's intervention in Yemen and its attack on Saudi borders alarmed many Arab states, particularly Syria, Jordan and Iraq. In response, these countries expressed their intention to prevent Nasser from expanding his authority throughout the region. Despite the fact that the Syrians earlier recognized the new republican regime, by late November 1962 the Syrians began characterizing al-Sallal, president of the Yemen Arab Republic (1962–1967), as a stooge of Nasser. They, along with the Jordanians, interpreted Nasser's move into Yemen as the first step in taking over Saudi Arabia. Further, they saw the threat to Saudi Arabia as presaging a threat to Syria and Jordan. Viewing Nasser's intentions in this manner, King Hussein of Jordan sent Jordanian military personnel to train Yemeni royalists in mine laying, guerilla warfare and in the use of light artillery. President Nasser, in a discussion with a special correspondent of *Foreign Reports Bulletin* on November 24, 1962, did not express much concern about Jordan's position; moreover, he admitted that:

> Egypt's policy was to support the progressive forces throughout the Arab world, and therefore would be bound to help the Yemeni revolution against the attempt to restore the Imamate system.

He went on to say, as the *Bulletin* paraphrased him, that:

> . . . it is certainly no secret that it is [Egyptian] forces which are doing the fighting in Yemen and that Egyptian forces hold Yemen as a whole.

Nasser then boasted, according to the *Bulletin*, that:

. . . if further action is necessary, Egyptian forces can reach Jeddah, the seaport of Saudi Arabia, in 24 hours, and that it also had two paratroop brigades that could be dropped in Saudi Arabia within two hours.

Nasser further asserted that he:

". . . could provoke trouble all over Saudi Arabia . . . around Jeddah, in the Eastern Province, and in the North, and all that is needed is for Cairo Radio to order demonstrations in the towns, due to the fact," he said, "that Cairo Radio is widely listened to in Saudi Arabia."[59]

All in all, and in varying degrees, the various factors discussed above contributed to the outbreak of Yemeni Civil War, which lasted for eight years (1962–1970). In fact, the war itself was principally an armed struggle between royalist and republican Yemeni factions, the former supported by Saudi Arabia through arms, supplies, financial and moral help, while the latter was supported by Egyptian military forces, financial and professional assistance.

If President Nasser had not interfered in Yemen, it seems likely that the Yemeni Civil War could have been prevented, and Yemenis could have solved their own internal disputes. But he did interfere, and that action was one which he and his closest political and military advisors lived to regret in June 1967. The bitter irony in this conflict which spanned eight years is that despite the great toll exacted by it in terms of human life and financial resources, not one of the three parties involved can claim to have gained anything. In fact, all three lost a great deal.

Notes

[1] Manfred W. Wenner, *Modern Yemen, 1918–1966* (Baltimore: The Johns Hopkins Press, 1967), p. 35.

[2] Hugh Scott, "The Yemen in 1937–38," *Journal of the Royal Central Asian Society*, vol. XXVII, part 1 (January 1940), pp. 22–23.

[3] Robert W. Stookey, *Yemen: The Politics of the Yemen Arab Republic* (Boulder, CO: Westview Press, 1978), p. 59.

[4] J. E. Peterson, *Yemen: The Search for a Modern State* (Baltimore: Johns Hopkins University Press, 1982), p. 172.

[5] Muhammad Sadiq Aql and Hiyam Abu Afiyah, *Adwa ala Thawrat al-Yaman* [Lights on the Yemen Revolution] (Cairo: Dar al-Qawmiyah lil-Tibaah wal-Nashr), p. 31.

[6] *Thawrat 26 Sibtambir: Dirasat wa Shahadat lil-Tarikh* [The September 26 Revolution: Studies and Evidence for History], 1st ed. 1981–82 (Beirut: Maktabat al-Jamahir, for Yemeni Center for Analysis and Studies, Sanaa), p. 18.

[7] Aql and Abu Afiyah, pp. 25, 27.

[8] Dr. Sayyid Mustafa Salim, *Takwin al-Yaman al-Hadith: al-Yaman wal-Imam Yahya (1904–1948)* [Structure of Modern Yemen: Yemen and Imam Yahya (1904–1948)], 3rd ed. (Cairo: Maktabat Medbouli, 1984), pp. 490–495.

[9] Ahmed Assah, *Muajizatun fawq al-Rimal* [A Miracle on the Sands], 2nd ed. (Beirut: Al-Matabi al-Ahliyah al-Lubnaniyah, 1966), p. 125.

[10] Edgar O'Ballance, *The War in Yemen* (London: Faber and Faber, 1971), p. 26.

[11] See text of interview, Appendix No. 4, Question and Answer Number 3.

[12] Lt. General Abdallah al-Guzaylan, *Al-Tarikh al-Sirri lil-Thawrah al-Yamaniyah* [The Secret History of the Yemen Revolution], 2nd ed. (Cairo: Maktabat Medbouli, 1979), pp. 12–15.

[13] Ibid, pp. 14, 16.

[14] Dr. Adnan Narsis, *Al-Yaman wa Hadarat al-Arab* [Yemen and Arab Civilization] (Beirut: Dar Maktabat al-Hayat, 1962), p. 163.

[15] Al-Guzaylan, p. 18. He was among the group of young that in early 1948 was sent first to Lebanon, then to Egypt and finally to the Soviet Union. He became a deputy prime minister, deputy high commander of the armed forces and member of the Revolutionary Council after the 1962 coup d'état.

[16] Interview with H.M. Imam Muhammad al-Badr, London: December 21, 1983, Appendix No. 2, Question and Answer Number 2.

[17] Robin Bidwell, *The Two Yemens* (Boulder, CO: Westview Press, 1983), p. 114.

[18] Abbas Faroughy, *Introducing Yemen* (New York: Orientalia, 1947), pp. 65–67.

[19] Ibid., p. 98.

[20] J. Heyworth-Dunne, "The Yemen," *Middle Eastern Affairs*, vol. IX, no. 2 (February 1958), p. 58.

[21] R. B. Serjeant, "The Two Yemens: Historical Perspectives and Present Attitudes," *Asian Affairs*, vol. 60, part 1 (February 1973), pp. 3–16.

[22] Narsis, p. 165.

[23] Sydney Nettleton Fisher, *The Middle East: A History* (New York: Knopf, 1959), p. 545.

[24] Interview with H.M. Imam Muhammad al-Badr, London: December 21, 1983, Appendix No. 2, Question and Answer Number 4. See also, Guzaylan.

[25] Ibid.

[26] See Harold Ingrams, *The Yemen* (New York: Praeger, 1964), pp. 164–169.

[27] Interview with H.M. Imam al-Badr, London: December 21, 1983, Appendix No. 2, Question and Answer Number 1.

[28] Ibid., Question and Answer Number 2.

[29] Edgar O'Ballance, *The War in Yemen* (London: Faber and Faber, 1971), p. 67.

[30] Interview with H.M. Imam al-Badr, London: December 21, 1983, Appendix No. 2, Question and Answer Number 3.

[31] Ingrams, p. 133.

[32] Interview with H.E. Mahmoud Riad, Cairo: November 11, 1984, Appendix No. 4, Question and Answer Number 1.

[33] In an interview with H.E. Mahmoud Riad on November 11, 1984, he stated: ". . . President Nasser relied totally on Anwar al-Sadat vis-à-vis the Yemen question. But al-Sadat himself relied on Abd al-Rahman al-Baidani and his analysis of the situation in Yemen." See Appendix No. 4, Question and Answer Number 3.

[34] Anwar al-Sadat, *In Search of Identity* (New York: Harper Colophon Books, 1978), p. 162.

[35] U.N. General Assembly Resolution 2131, adopted in 1965 and entitled Declaration on the Inadmissibility of Intervention in the Domestic Affairs of States and the Protection of Independence and Sovereignty, states: "No state has the right to intervene, directly or indirectly, for any reason whatever, in the internal or external affairs of any other state. Consequently, armed intervention and all other forms of interference or attempted threats against the personality of the state or against its political, economical, and cultural elements are condemned." See also, William B. O'Brien, *U.S. Military Intervention: Law and Morality* (Beverly Hills, CA: Sage Publications, 1979); The Center for Strategic and International Studies, Georgetown University, The Washington Papers, Number 68, Convention on Rights and Duties of States, December 26, 1933; and Charter of the Organization of American States, April 30, 1948, as amended by Protocol of Buenos Aires, February 27, 1967.

[36] Gerhard von Glahn, *Law Among Nations: An Introduction to Public International Law*, 4th ed. (New York: Macmillan Publishing Co., Inc., 1981), pp. 161–170.

[37] Stookey, pp. 231–232.

[38] Interview with H.E. Mahmoud Riad, Cairo: November 11, 1984. See Appendix No. 4, Question and Answer Number 1.

[39] A private Saudi source.

[40] Ingrams, p. 130.

[41] Wenner, p. 212.

[42] Air Force Pamphlet (AFP), Number 110–31, p. 5–7.

[43] Ibid.

[44] Ibid., p. 6-3.

[45] Ingrams, p. 132.

[46] *The New Republic*, vol. 149, August 3, 1963, p. 5.

[47] Christopher J. McMullen, *Resolution of the Yemen Crisis, 1963: A Case Study in Mediation* (Washington, DC: Institute for the Study of Diplomacy, School of Foreign Service, Georgetown University, 1980), p. 1.

[48] *The New York Times*, May 13, 1964, p. 5.

[49] Saudi Arabia began helping the Imam and his followers in April 1963. This was done in accordance with the Imam's personal request for King Saud's assistance.

[50] "The Times of London" as reported in *The New Republic*, vol. 149, August 3, 1963, p. 8.

[51] Robert Lacey, *The Kingdom: Arabia & the House of Sa'ud* (New York and London: Harcourt Brace Jovanovich Publishers, 1981), p. 346.

52 David Holden and Richard Johns, *The House of Saud* (New York: Holt, Rinehart and Winston, 1981), p. 569.

53 A Saudi official privately told the writer of this incident.

54 O'Ballance, pp. 97–98.

55 Ibid., pp. 125–126.

56 Interview with H.M. Imam Muhammad al-Badr, London: December 21, 1983, Appendix No. 2, Question and Answer Number 9.

57 *Foreign Reports Bulletin* (FRB), November 13, 1962, p. 2. This Bulletin is a confidential newsletter which is perhaps the most influential of those circulating among the major oil companies. It was published and written by both Harry Kern (an American businessman) and Samir Souki (a Lebanese political activist), in 1957. It is based in Washington, D.C.

58 FRB, November 30, 1962 (Interview with Nasser), p. 2.

59 At the time, Egypt had approximately 20,000 Egyptians serving in different cities of Saudi Arabia as teachers, doctors and technicians. At the same time, many Saudis, particularly the younger ones, were considered sympathetic to Nasser and his Pan-Arab movement. Many Saudi students were also studying in Cairo.

Chapter 4

THE SAUDI ROLE IN THE YEMEN CIVIL WAR

Fundamentally, Saudi involvement in the Yemen crisis was forced on the kingdom as a result of external involvement in the civil war. Initially, the kingdom sought to avoid becoming involved in Yemen's domestic affairs. However, its eventual policy *vis-à-vis* the Yemeni situation was determined in reaction to Egypt's support of the hostile republican regime in Sanaa and the threat to Saudi security perceptibly posed by Nasser and his Yemeni clients.

The Saudi involvement in the Yemeni dilemma had its roots in Arab rivalry. Between 1956 and 1965, the Arab world was engulfed in a bitter "cold war" that divided it into two distinct camps representing opposing ideologies. On the one side were the republics, established through military coups d'état, whose revolutionary ideologies espoused socialism and Pan-Arabism. The latter was associated with racial, linguistic and cultural unity, as well as with a proposed union of Arab states.[1] Largely by force of his personality, Egyptian President Gamal Abd al-Nasser became the *de facto* leader of this camp. Nasser used his position as head of the most populous and most modernized state in the Arab world to advance the notion that this radical Pan-Arab socialism of the revolutionary republic was the wave of the future and that similar republics would replace the "anachronistic" Arab monarchies and conservative republics. He announced that Egypt's new policy would be based on the principle of "unity of goals," meaning that Egypt could work closely only with other revolutionary countries that shared its major objectives.[2] Meanwhile, he broadened and enlarged Egypt's financial and moral support to various radical movements in the Arab world, and Cairo became the headquarters for most of these organizations.

Consequently, conservative Arab regimes found themselves on the defensive and looked upon Nasser and his fellow "progressives" as a threat to their own existence. Most of these conservative countries, including Saudi Arabia, Iraq (before 1958), Jordan, and Tunisia, aligned themselves with the major Western powers, namely, the United States, Britain and France, in order to deter, if not stop, Nasser from attacking and threatening the status quo.[3]

A principal instrument for Nasser's propaganda campaign against these conservative forces (as well as others who did not like his policy line such as Abd al-Karim Qasim in Iraq) was Radio Cairo's well-known "Voice of the Arabs." This radio broadcast was established in 1953 to encourage the myth of Arab nationalism and to inculcate the criteria by which the people could identify the "imperialist enemies in our midst," as Nasser put it.[4] Nasser's propaganda campaign was combined with the buildup of the Egyptian armed forces as important elements in advancing and achieving his political goals. Beginning in 1955, Nasser increased the amount of Egypt's resources that were devoted to the armed forces. Nasser's belief that Pan-Arabism was achievable and even probable was encouraged by the existence of the Arab League, the 1958 union between Egypt and Syria, and the association of Yemen with that union.

Nevertheless, implementation of the vision of Arab unity faced many obstacles, among them widely variant political systems and personal animosities between Arab leaders. Just as important was the widespread lack of political participation and even political consciousness on the part of the Arab masses. One writer estimates the proportion of the politically active population, concerned with Arab nationalism, at 20–25 percent in Egypt, Lebanon and Syria, some 10–15 percent in Jordan and Iraq, some 3–4 percent in the Sudan, and only a tiny percentage in Saudi Arabia, Yemen, and the other Gulf shaykhdoms.[5]

There are those pro-Nasserist Arab politicians, such as Mr. Mahmoud Riad, who are of the opinion that Nasser never attempted to achieve total and complete unity among Arab states and that he was only interested in and concerned with security arrangements.[6] But this view could be refuted, given Nasser's own words to Jean Lacouture:

> Listen to me: I have an exact knowledge of the frontiers of the Arab nation. I do not place it in the future for I think and I act as though it already existed. These frontiers end where my propaganda no longer arouses an echo. Beyond this point something else begins, a foreign world which does not concern me.[7]

As explained by Nasser himself, this line of policy forced the conservative Arab states to believe firmly that his motivation was Egyptian "imperialism" rather than a "national liberation" movement. At the same time, these conservative regimes regarded his activities as inter-ference in their internal affairs. Therefore, they had no choice but to unite together and coordinate their foreign policies. Toward this end, Saudi Arabia, Jordan and Iraq ended their longstanding animosity and reached a reconciliation in June 1957, and the Hashimi regimes in Iraq and Jordan announced their merger in late February 1958.[8] Other Arab states, such as Lebanon, preferred to remain neutral, and Yemen, under Imam Ahmad, joined the United Arab States in an attempt to outflank Nasser's criticism and propaganda.

The rivalries between the leaders of the Arab states continued, notwithstanding changes in their political systems. For instance, on July 14, 1958, a coup d'état in Iraq brought down the monarch. But not even this new progressive republican regime could coexist peacefully with Nasser and his dominating personality, and the two countries found themselves at odds as early as 1959. Two main factors contributed to this. First, both Iraq and Egypt emphatically stressed their own national interests. In fact, those interests were far more diverse than the popular slogans of Arab unity.[9] Second, while Egypt expected to assume leadership of the Arab unity movement, Iraqi nationalists were divided between those who favored complete Arab unity at once and those who favored a united Fertile Crescent state with Syria as a first step.[10] In 1961, Syria withdrew from the United Arab Republic, dealing a severe blow to Nasser and his ambitions. Syrian-Egyptian differences had arisen over Egyptian domination of an unequal union and over Syrian Baathist objection to Nasserist ideology. In a speech on October 16, 1961, Nasser admitted his problems, as he stated, "We must have the courage to confess our errors. We must blame ourselves for the collapse of the union with Syria." The Syrian experience, however, did not prevent Nasser from pursuing his revolutionary goals. On the contrary, it turned his attention to a new tactic, and made him believe that regeneration of the Arabs would never be accomplished, save through struggle and revolution.[11] From then on, Nasser began searching for a means to regain his lost prestige in the Arab world. North Yemen in 1962 provided such an opportunity. His ultimate objective, however, was not just Yemen but the entire Arabian Peninsula; and Yemen was only a foothold.[12]

Given Nasser's ideology, propaganda, and oft-expressed hostility, the Kingdom of Saudi Arabia had no choice but to act to counter Nasser's military intervention in North Yemen. In fact, Nasser's ideology and propaganda could be inferred from one of his speeches. On March 26, 1964, Nasser delivered a speech at the first meeting of the Eygptian National Assembly in Cairo, where he said:

The first enemy is imperialism, the second Israel . . . and the third the forces of reaction in the Arab world. . . . The separatist movement which arose in Damascus was able on September 28, 1961, to break up the union of Syria and Egypt; but the revolution in Yemen reversed this course and forced reaction to take the defensive.[13]

Moreover, Nasser embraced the old Egyptian belief in Egypt's centrality to the region around it and its supremacy and its urge to pursue its destiny in places such as the Sudan, Syria, and the Arabian Peninsula. Consequently, this kind of belief alarmed Saudi Arabia's leaders, whose forefathers had been driven out of the Arabian Peninsula in the early 19th century by Muhammad Ali Pasha and his son Ibrahim.[14] As Egyptian involvement in Yemen continued and intensified in the months following the coup, Saudi internal security and stability were becoming more and more precarious. Anti-Saudi propaganda emanated from both Egyptian and North Yemen radio stations, as well as from their print media.

From the Saudi point of view, Yemen was at the time and continues to be of immense importance to the internal security of Saudi Arabia. Thus, the stability and security of Yemen has been seen by the kingdom to be as essential as its own.

The Yemeni Dimension of Saudi Security Concerns Following the 1962 Coup d'Etat

Since its founding in 1932, the Kingdom of Saudi Arabia has had a remarkable record of internal security and stability, particularly for so volatile a region as the Middle East. To preserve this high degree of stability, Saudi Arabia necessarily has concerned itself with all real and potential subversive or insurgent activities occurring in neighboring countries, of which North Yemen is one. The stakes are high, not only for the kingdom but also for the Free World, which is interested in the uninterrupted flow of Saudi oil.[15]

The Egyptian intervention in Yemen in 1962 was viewed seriously by the kingdom. In particular, hostile statements made by the new republican regime in Yemen raised fears and alarm in the kingdom that it was about to experience a new dimension of inter-Arab rivalry at its southern doors. An Egyptian puppet government in Sanaa in the eyes of Saudi Arabia undoubtedly would threaten the internal security of the kingdom and create conditions of unrest among the Saudi people, particularly in the kingdom's Southern Province.[16] At the same time, the presence of Egyptian troops in Yemen was perceived by Saudi Arabia as an act of aggression aimed at more than merely controlling

Yemen or even driving the British from Aden and the protectorates. The troops were also seen as posing a direct threat to the existence of the kingdom, especially in view of Nasser's verbal attacks on monarchial systems in the Arab world, and his threat to attack Saudi territory.[17]

Saudi Arabia, according to a prominent Saudi politician dealing with Saudi policymaking towards North Yemen, could not keep silent or tolerate any external military or political interference in North Yemen.[18] According to him, this included all Arab states, particularly those who had tried to "shake" the political weight and strength of the kingdom in the Arab world. Their attempts to establish a sphere of influence inside Yemen would not be tolerated by the kingdom. During the Arab cold war, this applied especially to Egypt, Syria and Iraq. The position outlined by this influential Saudi politician indicated Saudi Arabia's determination and perceived right to defend itself and preserve its internal security and stability. Accordingly, the 1962 situation in Yemen was viewed as intolerable and the kingdom was left with no alternative but to defend itself against Nasser and his troops. In a speech in 1963, King Faisal recalled that:

> Egypt's rulers declared that they had sent their expeditions to fight in Yemen to destroy our country and capture it. We were, therefore, driven into a position where we had no alternative but to defend ourselves. Every state and every country in the world is entitled to self-defense.[19]

From the Saudi point of view, "revolutionary Yemen" in the 1960s was capable of exerting a negative influence on the kingdom directly or indirectly. One potential direct means of undermining the stability of the kingdom would be to use the Yemeni work force in Saudi Arabia to conduct acts of sabotage or to organize and promote underground activities. This, in fact, happened in 1963 when the republican regime in Yemen, encouraged by Nasser, paid some Yemenis working in the kingdom to carry out acts of sabotage inside the country.[20] A second direct action to destabilize the kingdom was also attempted in 1964 when a number of armed Yemeni infiltrators tried to cross the Yemen-Saudi border with the intention of damaging vital and strategic military and civilian targets. However, they were captured and executed by the Saudi authorities.[21]

The formation of an anti-Saudi government constituted an indirect negative influence that North Yemen could exert on Saudi stability. The republican government in 1962, by overthrowing the monarchy and setting up a republic, was an indirect negative influence which could affect Saudi stability because of the possible spillover effect caused by its example. Essentially, it tried to de-emphasize Saudi-Yemeni relations, and cooperated with an anti-Saudi regime, Egypt, in an effort to disrupt Saudi internal security. By intensifying border hostilities, the republican regime in Sanaa confirmed Saudi suspicions of its intentions, as well as those of Egypt. On November 16, 1962, Mohammed Hassanein Haikal wrote: "The victory of the Yemen Revolution, together with those in Saudi Arabia and Jordan, are all steps on the road towards total victory in Palestine."[22]

Against all these hostile actions and statements by both Egyptian and Yemeni officials, the Kingdom of Saudi Arabia became increasingly convinced that its security and stability were in danger. Egyptian attacks on Saudi border towns and teams of saboteurs infiltrated into the kingdom provided tangible justification of Saudi concerns. Therefore, the kingdom faced the necessity, as well as the right, to defend itself by all available means. Among those means was assistance to the deposed Imam of Yemen and his supporters.

Saudi Assistance to the Royalist Forces

Despite the fact that North Yemen is politically, economically, geographically and militarily, important to the Kingdom of Saudi Arabia, the September 26, 1962, coup d'état in that country was perceived by the kingdom as a "domestic affair" that should be solved by the Yemeni people themselves, without any outside interference either from Arab or non-Arab powers.[23] However, the kingdom was pushed to interfere and extend its political, financial and moral support to the ex-Imam and his followers as a result of three major factors: (1) the Egyptian air raids on Saudi border towns; (2) the hostile attitudes of the new republican regime in Sanaa towards the kingdom; (3) the constant aid requests by the Yemeni royal family.

The Egyptian Air Raids on Saudi Border Towns

Saudi Arabia closely monitored the Egyptian attitude toward and involvement with the new republican government in North Yemen. King Saud of Saudi Arabia, owing to illness, was frequently in Europe for long periods during much of 1962. Prince Faisal, Crown Prince at the time, was attending the Annual Meeting of the U.N. General Assembly in New York when the Yemeni coup d'état took place. When asked about the Yemeni coup d'état, Crown Prince Faisal answered that it was a Yemeni "domestic affair," and Saudi Arabia had nothing to do with it.[24] However, the Saudi position changed dramatically in the aftermath of the November 1962 Egyptian air attacks on Saudi border towns. The bombing of Saudi towns and villages was perceived by the kingdom as a dangerous step, particularly since the kingdom lacked sophisticated weapons and an air defense system to defend itself. Egyptian bombardments of Nijran, Jizan, Abha and Khamis Mushayt affected the residential areas, the water wells and the civilian roads. As a result of the attacks which took place in March 1963, 36 patients inside an Abha hospital were killed.[25] Undoubtedly these Egyptian attacks were working against President Nasser and in favor of Saudi Arabia in terms of world opinion, in general, and American public opinion, in particular.[26]

Frustrated by the defeat of Egyptian forces at the hands of the royalist forces inside Yemen and his unsuccessful attacks against the Saudi border towns, President Nasser turned to new tactics. These took the form of subversive activities inside the urban areas of Saudi Arabia. For example, in November 1962, Egyptian planes dropped arms inside the kingdom in the fanciful belief that they would be found and used by forces in opposition to Saudi rule. However, these weapons were actually captured by the Saudi security forces.[27]

On another track, by October 1962, Egyptian newspapers began castigating King Saud and threatening him about the fate awaiting him and the Saudi royal family in general.[28] Cairo Radio, too, attacked King Saud and admonished him against extending any kind of assistance to the counterrevolutionary forces headed by Prince al-Hasan of Yemen.[29] On October 23, 1962, Cairo Radio issued a warning to Crown Prince Faisal, asserting that "the sons of all the Arabian Peninsula lie in wait for you and your family . . . Faisal nothing but death awaits you."[30]

Such military actions and media campaigns continued throughout 1962 and early 1963. Against these developments, Saudi Arabia had no choice but to sever diplomatic relations with Egypt and prepare to defend its southern borders.

The Hostile Attitudes of the New Regime in Yemen
Towards Saudi Arabia

Despite Saudi Arabia's initial neutrality *vis-à-vis* the coup d'état in North Yemen, the new republican regime in Sanaa, relying largely on Egyptian military support, began to express hostile attitudes towards the Kingdom of Saudi Arabia. Instead of encouraging Saudi neutrality, let alone seeking its backing and support, Y.A.R. President Abdallah al-Sallal launched a hostile campaign against Saudi Arabia.[31] To wit, in October 1962, al-Sallal publicly announced his intention to extend a "republican form of government" to the entire Arabian Peninsula.[32] Moreover, on October 1, 1962, Abd al-Rahman al-Baydani, deputy prime minister of Yemen, called the Saudi chargé d'affaires in Sanaa and instructed him to leave the country.[33] In the meantime, he ordered the closure of the Yemeni legation in Saudi Arabia. In a speech on October 1, 1962, al-Baydani clearly expressed his antagonistic attitude:

> We have taken all measures to move the battle to the Saudi territory itself and to Riyadh itself, if necessary. This is not for local consumption or propaganda. In the name of the Government of the Yemeni Arab Republic and in the name of the Yemeni people, I declare the acceptance of the Saudi challenge. We shall wait for it to begin.[34]

In November 1962, President al-Sallal claimed that Jizan, Najran and the Province of Asir in the southwestern part of Saudi Arabia belonged to Yemen and should be returned to Yemen proper.[35] In the interim, al-Sallal's government assured the U.S. government that in the event of an Egyptian-Yemeni invasion of Saudi Arabia, Yemen would guarantee American installations in the Arabian Peninsula.[36] Obviously, this was an attempt to preserve the United States' neutrality in case the war were to spread to Saudi Arabia. However, it was "wishful thinking" on the part of the Yemeni republicans, who lacked even minimal power to control Yemen itself and who, in December 1962, dropped the idea of invasion and began talking only about bombing "strategic" targets inside Saudi Arabia.[37] This hostile Yemeni republican attitude against Saudi Arabia became a major factor in the April 1, 1963, Saudi decision to support the royalist forces. It is quite possible that Yemen's hostility was rooted in a fear of Saudi intervention. However, such a fear, if present, was without basis at this time. First, no royalist forces had been permitted to operate out of Saudi Arabia. Second, assistance in the form of financial support did not begin until April 1963.

Royalists' Aid Requests

In the aftermath of the new coup d'état and the concomitant falsified publicity about the death of Imam Muhammad al-Badr, his uncle al-Hasan, Yemen's representative at the United Nations, proclaimed himself as the new Imam of Yemen. On September 27, 1962, al-Hasan issued a statement to the Yemeni people from New York assuring them that he was on his way to Yemen to meet with them.[38] On September 30, 1962, the Saudi government permitted him to enter the kingdom, where he and other members of the Yemen royal family requested aid from King Saud. The king did not then commit himself to financial or material help, but assured them of his moral support.[39] From there, al-Hasan proceeded to the northern part of Yemen to begin his struggle against the republican regime. He also announced the formation of a "royalist government" in exile.[40] Approximately on October 8, 1962, Imam al-

Badr, who was believed dead by the republican regime in Sanaa, appeared and announced his plans to counter the rebels in Sanaa and regain his throne.[41]

Consequently, Prince al-Hasan renounced his claim to the Imamate and joined his efforts with Imam al-Badr, who proceeded to the Yemeni-Saudi border and sent a message to King Saud asking for assistance.[42] Despite the attitudes of the new rulers of Yemen, effective Saudi support was not forthcoming until April 1963, when the kingdom became fully convinced that both Egypt and the new republican regime in Sanaa were determined to destabilize Saudi Arabia and create unrest throughout the Arabian Peninsula.

The Nature of Saudi Assistance to the Royalist Forces

Before becoming fully engaged in assisting the Yemeni royalist forces led by Imam Muhammad al-Badr, his uncle al-Hasan, and other members of the Yemeni royal family, the Saudi monarchy had to take a number of measures to secure Saudi Arabia's southern border and defend it against possible Egyptian air attacks. These defensive measures were carried out in a number of ways. A general mobilization was ordered and army leaves were cancelled. Three squadrons of Saudi jets were dispatched to an air base near the Yemeni border, and antiaircraft guns were moved to the border region of Najran. A nominal number of Jordanian troops joined the Saudi troops stationed on the Yemen border.[43]

These defensive measures, however, were interpreted by Egypt and the republican regime in Sanaa as offensively aimed against them, as well as in favor of the royalist forces. As a matter of fact, Saudi Arabia never interfered militarily in Yemen. Its assistance to the royalist forces was limited to political, financial and moral assistance. Financial assistance included money for the purchase of arms. Inasmuch as it aimed at preserving Saudi Arabia's own integrity, this support was moral as well as defensive in nature.

Undoubtedly, if Egypt had not interfered in Yemen, the Yemen civil war could have been averted, and Saudi Arabia would not have been drawn into assisting the royalist forces. Historically, Saudi Arabia had been at odds with the Imams of Yemen. At a 1967 meeting at Khartoum, Sudan, aimed at resolving the Yemeni dilemma and arranged by the Sudanese premier, Muhammad Ahmad Mahjub, at his house, President Nasser raised the question of the Hamid al-Din family and Saudi help to them. King Faisal answered him: "Dear Gamal, the family of Hamid al-Din has been my enemy for forty years, not just a few years."[44]

Nevertheless, the Saudi decision to finance and support the royalist forces did not come until April 1963, a full six months after the Egyptians had bombarded Saudi border towns and Yemeni republicans were attacking the kingdom and its rulers. With Saudi assistance, however, the royalist forces succeeded in repulsing the Egyptian troops and pushed them back as far as the gates of Sanaa, the capital, at least temporarily.[45]

On September 5, 1963, Crown Prince Faisal spoke to a mass rally in the city of Taif, where he addressed the Saudi position *vis-à-vis* the Yemen dilemma and the status of Saudi assistance to the legitimate Imam and his royalist supporters:

> First, when this problem started, the Government and this country—and it is you, my fellow citizens who are the Government and the country— we all found ourselves in a position where we had no choice but to act according to our principles, our religion and our honour. We found ourselves in a position where we had no alternative but to defend ourselves and to defend our country.
>
> Egypt's rulers declared that they had sent their expedition to fight in Yemen to destroy our country and to capture it. We were, therefore, driven into a position where we had no alternative but to defend ourselves. Every state and every country in the world in entitled to self-defence.[46]

In another speech earlier that year, Faisal spoke at Mina near Makkah, where he explained the nature of the Saudi assistance to the royalist forces:

> Friends, with what do we help our brothers in the Yemen? If we are helping some of them with food and with other things to enable them to preserve their lives, would that be considered as assistance? We did not send fleets, planes and tanks to burn villages, houses, children and aged people. Nevertheless, we have offered to agree on the principle that all foreign forces in the Yemen be withdrawn. This done, we are willing to reach an agreement to stop assistance to the Yemen from every source and to leave to the Yemenis the freedom to decide their fate and the kind of government they wish to have.[47]

Throughout the Yemen crisis, Saudi Arabia insisted on implementing the principle of "self-determination" by the Yemeni people. When King Faisal was interviewed by Salim Habaji, the *al-Hayat* correspondent from Beirut, regarding a settlement for Yemen in November 1964, the following exchange occurred:

> *Habaji*: And what if you were asked to put forward a basis for a settlement?

King Faisal: I would say exactly the same thing, namely, that the Yemeni people alone have the right to determine their destiny and choose the type of government and rulers they want.[48]

Rather than deter Saudi Arabia from supporting the Yemenis, Egyptian actions in Saudi Arabia and in Yemen proper drew the kingdom—for self-defense and humanitarian reasons—into more direct support for the Yemeni royalists, a move that Saudi Arabia had been reluctant to make since the beginning of the crisis.

On the political front, Saudi Arabia made extensive efforts to explain its position in particular and the situation in general to various countries, and inside appropriate international and regional organizations. For example, on October 3, 1962, Crown Prince Faisal met with members of the U.S. Senate Foreign Relations Committee and mentioned, among other issues, the Egyptian intervention in Yemen.[49] On October 4, President Kennedy gave a lunch for the crown prince, which was followed by a private talk between the two. During that private talk with President Kennedy, the crown prince clarified a number of points in connection with the situation in Yemen and Saudi Arabia's position.[50] Essentially, the Saudi position was based on the following points: the new regime in Yemen depended on open and admitted Egyptian military intervention on a large scale; Imam al-Badr was not only alive but still in Yemen, supported by a considerable body of tribesmen—thus the legal government of Yemen was still in existence; and the new republican regime's first act was to execute any persons of political consequence in the country.

Moreover, the same Saudi position was also made clear to the British government. For its part, the British Government was considering three courses of action regarding Yemen: (1) to go along with the United States' position; (2) to support a revival of the Imamate system; or (3) to accept a prolonged struggle in Yemen between the republican and royalist forces.[51] As events later proved, they pursued the third course, if not by choice, being forced to adopt it as a result of Nasser's decision to broaden the war front by attacking Aden Protectorate. As a matter of fact, Saudi-British views of the Yemeni dilemma were much closer than Saudi-American views, particularly during the first two years of the Yemeni civil war. For example, the British did not recognize the republican regime in Sanaa although the United States did.

Saudi Arabia also intensified political contacts with several Arab states, particularly those which did not recognize the new republican regime in Sanaa. Among them were Jordan, Lebanon and Kuwait, who expressed their concern about the Egyptian role in Yemen. In the meantime, Saudi efforts inside the circles of the United Nations succeeded in October 1962 in preventing the U.N. secretary-general from accepting the credentials of the representatives of the new Yemeni regime.[52] Moreover, Saudi Arabia supported the royalists' case inside the Arab League, and when the League recognized the republican regime and accepted the credentials of its representatives on March 23, 1963, the kingdom objected to the move. However, it was outvoted.[53]

All in all, one may conclude that the Saudi role in the Yemen crisis and its resultant assistance to the royalist forces were dictated by external events. Attacks on Saudi border towns, threats to bring down the Saudi regime broadcast from Cairo Radio and similar threats reiterated by the republican president in Sanaa—factors perceptibly aimed at destabilizing the kingdom and thereby jeopardizing its security—led Saudi Arabia to conclude it had to support the royalist forces in order to defend its own sovereignty. The whole issue became a serious challenge for Saudi Arabia, to which, in hindsight, the kingdom responded successfully.

Notes

[1] Charles D. Cremeans, *The Arabs and the World: Nasser's Arab Nationalist Policy* (New York: Frederick A. Praeger, 1963), p. 61.

[2] John S. Badeau, *The American Approach to the Arab World* (New York, Evanston, London: Harper & Row, 1968), pp. 54–55.

[3] Peter Mansfield, *Nasser's Egypt* (Baltimore: Penguin Books, 1965), p. 86.

[4] Miles Copeland, *The Game of Nations* (New York: College Notes & Texts, 1969), p. 246.

[5] Cremeans, p. 89.

[6] Interview with H.E. Mahmoud Riad, Cairo: November 11, 1984, Appendix No. 4, Question and Answer Number 1.

[7] Michael C. Hudson, *Arab Politics: The Search for Legitimacy* (New Haven: Yale University Press, 1977), p. 241.

[8] The differences between Saudi Arabia and the other two monarchies stemmed from the Saudi-Hashimi rivalry of the early twentieth century. Sharif Husayn, grandfather of the Hashimi kings of Jordan and Iraq had been driven out of the Hijaz by King Ibn Saud in the late 1920s. Ghassan Salamah, *Al-Siyasah al-Kharijyah al-Saudiyah mundhu Am 1945* [Saudi Foreign Policy Since 1945] (Beirut: Muassasat Dar al-Rihani lil-Tibaah wal-Nashr, 1980), pp. 630–632.

[9] Badeau, p. 50.

[10] J. C. Hurewitz, *Middle East Politics: The Military Dimension* (New York, Washington, London: F. A. Praeger, 1969), p. 157.

[11] Malcolm H. Kerr, *The Arab Cold War: Gamal 'Abd al-Nasir and his Rivals, 1958–1970*, 3rd ed. (London: Oxford University Press, 1971), pp. 26–27.

[12] Copeland, p. 266.

[13] Hisham B. Sharabi, *Nationalism and Revolution in the Arab World* (New York, Cincinnati, Toronto, London, Melbourne: Van Nostrand Reinhold, 1966), p. 118.

[14] Fouad Ajami, *The Arab Predicament* (London, New York, New Rochelle, Melbourne, Sydney: Cambridge University Press, 1981), pp. 80–81.

[15] Anthony H. Cordesman, *The Gulf and the Search for Strategic Stability: Saudi Arabia, the Military Balance in the Gulf, and Trends in the Arab-Israeli Military Balance* (Boulder, CO: Westview Press, 1984), p. 3.

[16] Historically, the imams of Yemen considered the province of Asir, Najran and Jizan as part of Yemen proper. The issue was resolved in 1934 after the two countries went to war, in which the Saudis were able to conquer al-Hudaydah, the main seaport of Yemen, and force Imam Yahya to recognize formally the then-existing borders.

[17] Kerr, p. 111.

[18] A Saudi official.

[19] Speech at Taif, September 5, 1963, as quoted in Gerald de Gaury, *Faisal: King of Saudi Arabia* (London: Arthur Barker, 1966), p. 172.

[20] David Holden and Richard Johns, *The House of Saud* (New York: Holt, Rinehart & Winston, 1981), p. 250.

[21] Seventeen Yemeni saboteurs were captured and executed. Robert Lacey, *The Kingdom: Arabia & the House of Sa'ud* (New York: Avon Books, 1981), p. 381.

[22] *Al-Ahram*, November 16, 1962.

[23] De Gaury, p. 162.

[24] *Foreign Reports Bulletin* (FRB), October 12, 1962, p. 1.

[25] Lacey, p. 246.

[26] C. J. McMullen, *Resolution of the Yemen Crisis, 1963: A Case Study in Mediation* (Washington, DC: Institute for the Study of Diplomacy, School of Foreign Service, Georgetown University, 1980), p. 1.

[27] Fred Halliday, *Arabia Without Sultans* (New York: Vintage Books, 1975), p. 121.

[28] *Al-Ahram*, October 1, 1962.

[29] BBC, *Summary of World Broadcast* (SWB), Part 4, October 20, 1962, p. 9.

[30] SWB, October 29, 1962, p. 4.

[31] Abdallah al-Sallal had been imprisoned several times by Imam Ahmad of Yemen for his opposition to the Imamate. When Imam Ahmad died on September 19, 1962, Prince Fahd ibn Abd al-Aziz (then minister of education and currently the king of Saudi Arabia) led the Saudi delegation to console the new Imam of Yemen. Among those Prince Fahd met was al-Sallal, who, according to Prince Fahd, expressed a kind of hatred when he shook hands with him.

[32] Manfred W. Wenner, *Modern Yemen: 1918–1966* (Baltimore: The Johns Hopkins Press, 1967), p. 195.

[33] Interview with Mr. Muhammad ibn Ajrumah, a Yemeni official who played important political roles throughout the Yemeni civil war. He was affiliated with the royalist forces.

[34] SWB, October 3, 1962, p. 3.

[35] FRB, November 13, 1962, p. 1.

[36] Ibid., p. 2.

[37] Ibid., December 5, 1962, p. 2.

[38] *The Times* (London), September 28, 1962.

[39] A high-ranking Saudi official.

[40] SWB, October 8, 1962, p. 3.

[41] Edgar O'Ballance, *The War in the Yemen* (London: Faber & Faber, 1971), pp. 78–79.

[42] Interview with H.M. Imam Muhammad al-Badr in London on December 21, 1983. See Appendix No. 2, Question and Answer Number 6.

[43] For more details of the Saudi defensive measures, see O'Ballance, pp. 95–96.

[44] Muhammad Ahmad Mahjub, *al-Dimuqratiyah fil-Mizan* [Democracy in the Balance] (Beirut: Dar al-Nahda, 1973), p. 172.

[45] Marill Gros, *Feisal of Arabia: The Ten Years of Reign* (England: EMG'E, SPIX, 1976), p. 105.

[46] De Gaury, p. 172.

[47] Ibid., p. 163.

[48] Ibid., p. 137.

[49] FRB, October 12, 1962, p. 2.

[50] Ibid., p. 1. Mr. Isa Sabbagh, from the American embassy in Saudi Arabia, acted as an interpreter.

[51] FRB, November 13, 1962, p. 2. At the time of the Yemen coup d'état, Saudi Arabia and Britain had no diplomatic relations. Relations had been severed over the two countries' dispute over the Buraimi oasis. However, relations were resumed in December 1962.

[52] FRB, October 10, 1962, p. 2.

[53] Butrus Butrus Ghali, *Al-Jamiah al-Arabiyah wa Taswiyat al-Munazaat al-Mahalliyah* [The Arab League and the Resolution of Local Disputes] (Cairo: n.p., 1977), p. 116.

Chapter 5

THE SUPERPOWERS' ROLE AND
INVOLVEMENT IN THE YEMEN DILEMMA

As often is the case in international relations, outside powers played key roles in Yemen's civil war. Among those powers were the United States of America and the Soviet Union. For its part, the United States assumed a double role. First, it served as a mediator between Saudi Arabia and Egypt, the principal external parties involved in the conflict. Second, the United States conducted limited military operations to discourage any further deterioration of peace in the area. The Soviet Union, for its part, supported Nasser's policies in Yemen and provided him with military equipment to support his adventure in Yemen. At the same time, the Soviets provided political, technical, economic, and military aid to the new republican regime in Yemen.

The superpowers, in fact, have long had their own interests in the Middle East in general, and in the Arabian Peninsula in particular. Consequently, those interests were largely responsible for determining the direction and scope of their actions throughout the Yemeni dilemma. Mr. Mahmoud Riad confirmed this view concerning the Soviets' goal in Yemen:

> It is a fact that each country looks after its own interests, and no one can argue this point. . . . During the Yemen Crisis, the Russians did not offer any opinions, and did not bargain with us. Their main goal was to find a foothold in Yemen. This, therefore, made them more willing to supply Egypt's needs in Yemen without condition.[1]

Nevertheless, superpower involvement in Yemen marked the second occasion of overt superpower rivalry in the Middle East since the end of World War II, the first being Iran in 1946. As a result, what had been a local, regional issue acquired global importance. While the policy objective of the United States was to cool the tension between Saudi Arabia and Egypt, the Soviet Union sought to encourage the Egyptian military involvement and strengthen the republican regime in Yemen.

Although both superpowers exercised considerable restraint, neither was ready to sacrifice its prestige and allow the other to gain any significant victory, either militarily or politically. The Yemeni dilemma, in fact, became a test for both powers. It showed Saudi Arabia and other moderate countries in the region just how far the United States was ready to stand by its friends. It also demonstrated to Egypt and the other revolutionary regimes the commitment of the Soviet Union in support of their revolutionary and progressive movements.

The United States' Role

The United States displayed its dual mediatory and military role in the Yemen situation from the beginning of the conflict. In fact, the Kennedy administration was approached early on by Crown Prince Faisal. On October 3 and 4, 1962, Crown Prince Faisal briefed the president and the Senate Foreign Relations Committee on the situation in Yemen and the Saudi position in that regard. The move by Crown Prince Faisal was successful in postponing U.S. recognition of the new regime in Yemen. It also contributed to President Kennedy's decision soon after to mediate between Saudi Arabia and Egypt in their conflict over North Yemen. The president's action took the form of messages sent on November 25, 1962, to Crown Prince Faisal, King Hussein, President Nasser, and President Abdallah al-Sallal, proposing a settlement of the conflict.[2] The chief points of his proposal were that:

1. The Egyptian troops would "gradually but promptly" withdraw from Yemen;
2. Saudi and Jordanian forces concentrated on the Yemeni border would "gradually but promptly" withdraw;
3. Some neutral body or third party would be brought in to guarantee that these measures were carried out—the United Nations might play a role;
4. The Sallal regime would recognize its international obligations and would negotiate with other elements in Yemen to stabilize the situation in that country; and
5. The United States would recognize the Sallal government and extend aid to it.[3]

However, only President al-Sallal accepted the proposal, and both Saudi Arabia and Egypt rejected it outright.[4] In a private interview with the correspondent of *Foreign Reports Bulletin* in Riyadh on

November 26, 1962, Crown Prince Faisal acknowledged receipt of President Kennedy's message but asserted that he had not as yet formally answered it.[5] He also strongly opposed any further recognition of the revolutionary regime in Yemen.[6] He further explained that this was exactly the kind of proposal that Nasser wanted, and his information indicated that the United States probably would announce recognition of the republican regime in any event.[7]

Crown Prince Faisal's prediction was accurate. On December 19, 1962, the United States recognized the republican regime in Yemen.[8] Washington officials tried to justify why that decision was taken and the following explanations were given: (1) It was felt that the revolutionary regime controlled the greater part of Yemen; (2) The royalists were thought to exercise control only in the border regions of the north and east; (3) The Egyptians would soon be able to withdraw without much fear that the tribes could upset the new government; (4) The administration feared that the Russians would move in under the guise of giving economic aid to Yemen; (5) It was also feared that the U.S. economic aid mission would be forced out of Yemen unless recognition was accorded soon.[9]

Saudi Arabia, notwithstanding anticipation of this decision by the United States, quickly expressed its displeasure. In fact, the Saudi objection to the U.S. action turned on the belief that recognition had been accorded without clear assurances that the Egyptian troops definitely would be evacuated and that all foreign intervention would cease. Moreover, Saudi Arabia viewed the U.S. action as recognition of Egypt's right to intervene in any part of the Arab world.[10]

The United Nations and fifty other countries followed the United States in recognizing the republican regime in Yemen. This prompted the United States to further justify its action as aimed at preventing an escalation of the Yemen conflict, which would cause even more foreign interference and place major U.S. economic and security interests in the Arabian Peninsula in serious jeopardy.[11] However, it seemed, at the time, that the U.S. action was also aimed at enabling the U.S. government to play an effective role in the mediation efforts.

U.S. mediation efforts in Yemen began as early as 1963, when Washington sent Ambassador Ellsworth T. Bunker to carry out negotiations between Saudi Arabia and Egypt. In the meantime, the U.S. government proposed to appoint a U.N. representative to the Middle East who would attempt to find a solution to the Yemen conflict under the aegis of the United Nations secretary-general. The United States in fact suggested the name of an Italian diplomat, Ambassador Pier Pasquale Spinelli, who had served previously as U.N. special representative to the Middle East in 1958. The proposal was turned down, however, by

Secretary-General U Thant, who allegedly was sensitive to charges that he was too closely aligned with American interests. The Soviets, along with other communist countries and other radical governments, made these charges.[12] To strengthen reception of its mediation efforts, the United States provided the new republican regime in Yemen with $33 million in aid to be spent on a municipal water system in Taiz, an unpaved highway, and self-help irrigation programs. Nevertheless, President Abdallah al-Sallal complained at the amount, retorting that he had expected greater generosity from such a rich country.[13]

Ambassador Bunker's mission focused on reducing tension between Saudi Arabia and Egypt. He met individually with both Crown Prince Faisal and President Nasser and presented an American proposal that outlined a "disengagement agreement" between the two countries.[14] On April 10, 1963, and after a difficult series of "shuttle diplomacy" flights between Riyadh and Cairo, Ambassador Bunker was successfully able to secure the agreement of Egypt and Saudi Arabia to the following terms:

1. The Government of Saudi Arabia would terminate all support and aid to the royalists of Yemen and would prohibit the use of Saudi Arabian territory by royalist leaders for carrying on the struggle in Yemen;

2. Simultaneously with the suspension of Saudi Arabian aid to the royalists, the United Arab Republic would undertake to begin the phased withdrawal from Yemen of troops sent there to help the new government;

3. The United Arab Republic would not take punitive action against the royalists of Yemen for any resistance mounted by them prior to the beginning of this disengagement, and action on Saudi Arabian territory by U.A.R. forces would also end;

4. A demilitarized zone was to be established to a distance of 20 kilometers on each side of the demarcated Saudi Arabian-Yemen border;

5. Impartial observers were to be stationed in that zone to check on the observance of the terms of disengagement; they would also travel beyond the demilitarized zone, as necessary, to certify the suspension of activities in support of the royalists from Saudi Arabian territory and the outward movement of United Arab Republic forces and equipment from Yemen air and sea ports.[15]

On April 12, 1963, Ambassador Bunker returned to the United States and briefed the U.N. secretary-general on his mission. The latter agreed to accept the mission and began the necessary legal machinery required by U.N. rules and regulations.

The U.S. role in the Yemeni crisis, including some limited military action, assumed several forms. Saudi Arabia was provided with nominal military assistance, and cautious moves were made to deter the Soviet Union from expanding its involvement in Yemen. In this regard, when Egyptian planes bombed Saudi border towns in 1962 and 1963, the United States issued policy statements condemning these acts and expressing its serious concern.[16] In addition, the United States sent a squadron of jet fighters to Saudi Arabia in 1963 as a signal to both the Egyptians and the Soviets that the security of the kingdom was important to the United States and the West. A U.S. destroyer also was dispatched to Saudi Arabia to demonstrate support. At the same time, Saudi Arabia and the United States agreed upon an assistance program to help the kingdom to improve its air force capabilities.[17]

In the final analysis, one may say that the dual role of the United States during the Yemeni dilemma was productive in the search for a suitable solution of the problem. However, a lingering difficulty confronting U.S. allies, such as Saudi Arabia, remains the discontinuity of U.S. policies. For example, when the Yemeni conflict erupted in 1962, the United States appeared to be in the process of changing its position toward the so-called progressive and revolutionary regimes of the area in a belief that they would be the long-term "winners" in the region, and that monarchial regimes in Saudi Arabia and Jordan would not be able to stand the pressures and might fall within a few years.[18] This mindset and resultant shift in American policies constituted a serious problem for its Arab allies. In a private interview on December 22, 1962, Crown Prince Faisal opined that American policy seemed to him completely unrealistic; he felt that he has been let down by his American friends, and when he returned from the U.S. he felt very confident that the U.S. government understood the situation and that recognition of al-Sallal would only come after UAR forces had evacuated or agreed to a simultaneous disengagement.[19] Hence, as the preceding quote makes clear, Crown Prince Faisal was disappointed with the early U.S. response to the Yemeni crisis. Nevertheless, he continued to work with the United States in order to forge a policy more in line with Saudi interests.

The Soviet Union's Role

In examining the Soviet Union's role in the Yemen crisis, it becomes apparent that Moscow's involvement was deeper than that of the United States. This is not surprising, since the Soviet Union historically has found itself in an inferior position in the Middle East and therefore actively has sought to undermine existing American advantages there. Consequently, the Soviets have consistently exploited tensions in the area to advance their goals.

The combination of global and regional interests have fostered a two-level Soviet approach to the region. On the global level, the Soviets see the Middle East as only one arena in the broader struggle to supplant Western influence with Soviet-dominated Marxism. The Middle East, due to its geostrategic location, vital economic resources, and political and military significance, occupies a special place in the Soviet Union's Third World strategy. On a regional level, through exploitation, the Soviet Union seeks to manipulate anticolonial revolutions and radical revolts against traditional regimes, as well as the Arab-Israeli conflict, to enhance Soviet influence.[20]

This strategy became particularly evident after Nikita S. Khrushchev came to power in the 1950s, when he and his colleagues began to identify with national liberation philosophy, postcolonial nation-building process, and the growing need for economic development in the Third World. To gain influence in these countries, Moscow provided about $4 billion in economic credits and grants between 1954 and 1964, and military assistance, mostly in the form of long-term credits, was extended to approximately 15 countries.[21] By the mid-1960s, the Soviets had succeeded in projecting Soviet power and influence into the Third World, cheaply.[22]

In the Middle East, the Soviet Union concentrated policy attention on the southern sector (the Arab East and Israel) and worked to support Arab independence movements and their demands in 1946 and 1947 for withdrawal of Western troops from the area. The Soviets also supported the establishment of a Jewish state in Palestine. Then, in the aftermath of the 1967 Arab-Israeli War, the Soviet Union broke diplomatic relations with Israel and helped rebuild Egypt's military forces, which earned it the gratitude of much of the Arab world as a defender of Arab causes.[23]

The emergence of national and revolutionary regimes in the Arab world has created a two-level tactical approach as well. On the one hand, the Soviets have attempted to cooperate directly with radical new regimes, for example, Egypt in 1955 and Yemen in 1962. On the other hand, the Soviets also have pursued a policy of strengthening local communist and other radical leftist parties. These two-level approaches have, in fact, resulted sometimes in a conflict between Soviet support for the central regime and for the local communist parties.[24]

The Soviets try to increase their influence in many ways including arms transfers, economic projects with heavy political content (e.g., the high dam in Egypt), ideological persuasion, manipulation of local communist parties, support for subversive organizations, political and diplomatic support for national governments and political movements directed against the West, and a network of treaties and agreements of political and military cooperation, sometimes including the use of military facilities.[25] Despite their extensive efforts, the Soviets have had only mixed success in their attempts to increase their influence in the Middle East. They have scored successes with important crucial political and military assistance on critical occasions in the past and almost certainly will continue to play similar crucial roles in the future. However, they have also suffered repeated and severe frustration at the hands of their Middle East clients.[26]

Soviet interest in the Arabian Peninsula derives from various strategic objectives regarding this geographically, politically, militarily and economically important area. These objectives are:

1. To neutralize or eliminate Western military power and political influence in the Gulf and the Indian Ocean areas.

2. To create friendly allied states throughout the Gulf.

3. To transform the Gulf states into revolutionary states conforming to Soviet ideology.

4. To exploit the conflicts and tensions with the West and its allies in the region.

5. To expand Soviet influence to the surrounding states that affect Gulf security and enlarge its ability to threaten or control both the various oil shipment routes and other Western sources of oil and strategic minerals.

6. To build up Soviet military power in the region and Soviet power-projection capabilities.[27]

Two principal theories proffer explanation for Soviet policy towards the Arabian Peninsula as a whole. The first suggests that Moscow's policy is determined by a "grand design," a classic combination of strategy and tactics aimed at expanding Soviet interests in the area, as well as eroding the Western and Chinese presence. This theory is supported by those who argue that the real objective of the Soviet Union in the Arabian Peninsula is to "control the West's largest reservoir of oil in the Gulf." This rationale discounts the ultimate importance of Afghanistan, Iran or Pakistan to the Soviet Union, although these countries could be used by the Soviets as stepping-stones. The primary goal, according to this view, is Saudi Arabia.[28] Nevertheless, the Soviets wish to avoid war with the West over this vital area and also to avoid alienating the Arabian Peninsula states against them or their client states.[29]

The second theory holds that Soviet policy is merely "muddling through" in the area. According to this view, the Arabian Peninsula has been of only peripheral interest to Moscow. Consequently, the U.S.S.R. has not pursued any set policy for dealing with the area and has relied on "expedience and opportunism as the basis of its behavior, trying to take advantage of each opportunity for short- or long-term Soviet gain which has presented itself."[30] The situation in Yemen in 1962 provides a good example of this attitude. Essentially, the Soviet role in the Yemeni dilemma was conducted in a manner that would ensure its interests in the area and guarantee a substantial influence in Yemen proper. Consequently, Moscow recognized the new republican regime in Yemen on September 29, 1962, only three days after the coup d'état had taken place. Recognition was followed by various kinds of assistance to Yemen, including technical aid, military aid (including direct participation in air combat operations)[31] and political and financial support. Moscow also announced on October 15, 1962, that any country actively siding with the "counterrevolutionaries" would have to reckon with the Soviet Union.

By November 1962, the Soviets had sent 450 technicians to Sanaa, of whom some sixty were military technicians.[32] In the same month, a Yemeni military mission arrived in Moscow to seek more arms and Soviet help. The visit lasted for one week, during which the mission conferred with the Soviet Defense Minister Marshal Rodion Y. Malinoveski.[33] Importantly, the visit resulted in the signing of two agreements between Sanaa and Moscow in December 1962 for developing projects ranging from agriculture and water and power generators to factories, banks and radio.[34] By June 1963, it was reported that Soviet military technicians and instructors in Yemen had increased to 900 or 1,000.[35] By July 1963, it was reported that about 500 Soviet technicians were constructing a modern jet airport for Yemen under a $20 million development loan.[36]

The Soviet strategy in Yemen appeared to be aimed at establishing a sphere of influence in the Arabian Peninsula. Soviet control of Yemen not only would out-flank the oil fields but would also give the Soviets a base of operations near Britain's large military base in Aden, just across the Red Sea from East Africa. The pace of military, economic, and financial assistance increased and led to a state visit by President al-Sallal to Moscow in March 1964. There he signed a five-year treaty of friendship with the Soviets. In fact, there was another important reason for the visit: al-Sallal's belief that Nasser might abandon him and the republic, particularly after the unsuccessful efforts by Egyptian troops to wipe out the royalists. But Nasser was not contemplating loosening his grip over Yemen and visited Yemen in April 1964.[37] The purpose of Nasser's visit was to reassert his position in Yemen and to reassure al-Sallal that he intended to play a decisive and forceful role in Yemen. In addition, Nasser, by the visit, intended to boost the morale of Egyptian soldiers there.

President al-Sallal's visit to Moscow also achieved several other gains in addition to the friendship treaty:

1. An increase in economic and technical assistance to Sanaa;
2. An increase in the number of Soviet experts in different fields;
3. Additional arms shipments to Sanaa, reaching a high point in 1966;
4. The delivery of Soviet tanks and aircraft to Sanaa by 1964;
5. Soviet construction of the new harbor of al-Hudaydah; and
6. Soviet construction of high schools and paved roads.[38]

Despite their "undeclared" commitment to the protection and maintenance of the republican regime in Yemen, the Soviets sought to establish "unofficial" talks with the Imam Muhammad al-Badr, who was leading the "counterrevolutionary" royalist forces. In 1964, two representatives of the Red Cross, who had come to visit the battleground and investigate the alleged Egyptian use of napalm, met with the Imam. There the Swiss representative handed him a note bearing a request to see him alone. During this meeting, the Swiss representative informed the Imam of the Soviets' desire to begin negotiations with him. The Imam replied that he was ready to talk to the Soviets if a Soviet representative were to be sent to ask him officially to negotiate.[39] Apparently, the Soviets did not want to negotiate openly and therefore never sent their representative to the Imam.

The attempt to negotiate secretly with the Imam indicates the Soviets' concern for not annoying Nasser and the republican regime in Sanaa. Furthermore, the Soviet Union, like Egypt, had thought originally that Imam al-Badr had been killed. When he physically appeared, Moscow seemed to be less willing to support a military junta against a leader with whom it had had good relations in the past and who was responsible for bringing the Soviets into Yemen in the first place. At the same time, their deep involvement in supporting and financing Nasser's adventure in Yemen was becoming more and more costly. Soviet supplies of equipment and direct financial aid to Nasser's forces in Yemen reached the equivalent of $460 million.[40]

According to Imam al-Badr, Soviet troops also participated extensively in combat operations in Yemen, particularly following the Egyptian forces' withdrawal in late 1967. This Soviet military involvement was confirmed on December 10, 1967, when royalist forces shot down a republican MiG, which had been attacking their positions north of Sanaa, and discovered a dead Soviet pilot in the wreckage.[41] The Soviet Union, by supplying arms and pilots, was also instrumental in breaking the 1967–1968 siege of Sanaa.[42] Undoubtedly, this entailed a serious development that created considerable diplomatic stir in both Washington and Riyadh. In the meantime, the episode confirmed Soviet intentions and their strategy of infiltration and dominance over the troubled areas in the Middle East, in particular the Arabian Peninsula.

In sum, both superpowers became involved in the Yemeni conflict from its inception in September 1962. However, while the dual role of the United States was aimed principally at mitigating the situation and promoting a "disengagement agreement" between the two major outside parties to the conflict—Saudi Arabia and Egypt—the Soviet Union attempted to exploit the situation militarily by supporting both the new republican regime and Nasser's policies in Yemen. Moscow's role undoubtedly contributed to prolonging the crisis and in the process strengthened Nasser's determination to win that "unwinnable" war.

In spite of the extensive Soviet role in the Yemeni Civil War, the level of Soviet involvement in the Arabian Peninsula's political and military affairs has remained dependent on two major elements, namely, the extent of U.S. political and military presence in the vicinity and the degree of stability in the region.

Notes

[1] Interview with H.E. Mahmoud Riad, Appendix No. 4, Question and Answer Number 5.

[2] *Foreign Reports Bulletin* (FRB), December 5, 1962, p. 1.

[3] Ibid.

[4] Manfred W. Wenner, *Modern Yemen* (Baltimore: The Johns Hopkins Press, 1967), p. 199.

[5] FRB, December 5, 1962, pp. 1–2.

[6] Ibid.

[7] Ibid.

[8] J. B. Kelly, "The Future in Arabia," *International Affairs*, vol. 41 (October 1966), p. 638.

[9] FRB, December 5, 1962, p. 4.

[10] FRB, December 26, 1962, p. 1.

[11] This explanation was mentioned in a letter addressed to Senator Bourke B. Hickenlooper of Iowa by U.S. Assistant Secretary Phillips Talbot in early August 1963. Hickenlooper had written to Secretary of State Dean Rusk demanding withdrawal of U.S. recognition of the republican regime in Yemen. FRB, August 5, 1963.

[12] Christopher J. McMullen, *Resolution of the Yemen Crisis 1963: A Case Study in Mediation* (Washington, DC: Institute for the Study of Diplomacy, School of Foreign Service, Georgetown University, 1980), p. 7.

[13] *Newsweek*, "Revolutionary Gains," April 3, 1967.

[14] McMullen, p. 27.

[15] *United Nations Review*, vol. 10, no. 5 (May 1963), p. 1.

[16] *Middle East Affairs*, Vol. 14 (1963), p. 288.

[17] McMullen, p. 42.

[18] Under the Kennedy administration, the United States tried to find a new style of conduct and diplomacy which would convey its support for the independence and progress of the peoples of the emerging nations. Moreover, there was increasing awareness of the importance of accepting and making the most of the Afro-Asian revolution, in the statements of the president and some of his principal lieutenants, and in conduct of U.S. relations with the new nations. For more details, see Charles D. Cremeans, *The Arabs and The World: Nasser's Arab Nationalist Policy* (New York, London: Frederick A. Praeger, 1963), pp. 312–317 & p. 325.

[19] FRB, December 26, 1962, pp. 1–2.

[20] See John C. Campbell, "Soviet Strategy in the Middle East," and Stephen Page, "Moscow and the Arabian Peninsula," *American-Arab Affairs*, no. 8 (Spring 1984).

[21] Murray Gordon, ed., *Conflict in the Persian Gulf* (New York: Facts on File, 1981), pp. 45–46.

[22] By contrast, the United States between 1946 and 1965 provided $100 billion of economic and military assistance to less-developed areas. Gordon, p. 46.

[23] Bernard Reich, "The Soviet Union and the Middle East," *Social Science and Policy Research*, vol. II, no. 2 (December 1980), p. 50.

[24] Arnold Hottinger, "Arab Communism at Low Ebb," *Problems of Communism*, vol. 30 (July-August 1981), p. 18.

[25] John C. Campbell, "The Soviet Union in the Middle East," *The Middle East Journal*, vol. 32, no. 1 (Winter 1978), pp. 1–12.

[26] One such humiliating setback came when the Soviets were expelled from Egypt in 1972 by the late President Anwar al-Sadat.

[27] Anthony H. Cordesman, *The Gulf and the Search for Strategic Stability: Saudi Arabia, the Military Balance in the Gulf, and Trends in the Arab-Israeli Military Balance* (Boulder, CO: Westview Press; London: Mansell Publishing, 1984), pp. 78–79.

[28] Robert Moss, "Reaching for Oil: The Soviets' Bold Mideast Strategy," *Saturday Review*, vol. 7, no. 8 (April 12, 1980), p. 15.

[29] Cordesman, p. 79.

[30] David Lynn Price, "Moscow and the Persian Gulf," *Problems of Communism*, vol. 38 (March-April 1979), p. 2.

[31] Ibrahim al-Shurayqi, *Al-Sira al-Dami fil-Yaman* [The Bloody Conflict in Yemen], 1st ed. (n.p.: August 1964), p. 87.

[32] *The New York Times*, June 16, 1963.

[33] *Newsweek*, November 26, 1962.

[34] Harold Ingrams, *The Yemen: Imam, Rulers, and Revolution* (New York: Praeger, 1964), p. 137.

[35] *The New York Times*, June 16, 1963.

[36] Ingrams, p. 137.

[37] Manfred W. Wenner, *Modern Yemen: 1918–1966* (Baltimore: The Johns Hopkins Press, 1967), pp. 212–213.

38 Marshall I. Goldman, *Soviet Foreign Aid* (New York, 1967), p. 149; and Charles B. McLane, *Soviet–Middle East Relations* (London, 1973), p. 57.

39 Interview with H.M. Imam Muhammad al-Badr, London: December 21, 1983, Appendix No. 2, Question and Answer Number 12.

40 J. C. Hurewitz, *Middle East Politics: The Military Dimension* (New York: Praeger, 1969), p. 259.

41 Aryeh Y. Yodfat, *The Soviet Union and the Arabian Peninsula* (London: Croom Helm, 1983), p. 4.

42 J. E. Peterson, *Yemen: The Search for a Modern State* (Baltimore: The Johns Hopkins University Press, 1982), p. 102.

Chapter 6

THE END OF THE SAUDI-EGYPTIAN CONFLICT AND THE YEMEN CIVIL WAR

The Yemen crisis became so complex that the conflict dragged on for years. Mediation attempts extended some seven years (1963–1970) before peace could be restored. In fact, more than five consecutive years were spent in constant mediation efforts; these involved both international and regional organizations, as well as a number of Arab and non-Arab countries including the United States. None of these efforts, however, was directly responsible for eventually bringing an end to the Yemeni dilemma. The single most important factor occurred in 1967, when Egypt was forced to withdraw its troops from Yemen because of the Arab-Israeli War of June 1967. Even so, three more years were necessary before the Yemeni Civil War finally came to an end, largely through the mediation efforts of Saudi Arabia.

The primary focus of mediation efforts conducted before June 1967 was not on the republican and royalist forces but on their primary supporters, Egypt and Saudi Arabia. Major attempts at mediation were initiated by the Arab League, the United Nations, the United States, Kuwait, Sudan and Saudi Arabia (after 1967). Some of these initiatives were more successful than others, but none ultimately brought peace to Yemen, save for the Saudi initiative. That succeeded, partly, as a result of royalist and republican realization that the time had come for settling their eight-year-long bloody dispute.

The Arab League Mediation Efforts

The Arab League was seen at its establishment in 1945 as the first forum to which its members could turn in order to discuss and perhaps resolve their bilateral disputes. In the meantime, the organization was also supposed to act immediately upon the request of the disputed parties to bring a crisis under control and to prevent any further deterioration of the situation. This failed to occur in the case of Yemen in 1962, due largely to the fact that member states of the League were divided over which side to recognize as Yemen's proper representative government.[1] But this indecision did not preclude the secretary-general of the League from carrying out his responsibility in accordance with the League's Charter, which provides in Article Six that:

> If an act of aggression takes place by a member state of the League or one is feared, the victim or the threatened country may request an immediate meeting of the League Council. The Council will decide upon the necessary measures to deter the aggression. . . .[2]

Moreover, according to Article Eight of the League's Charter:

> Each participant state of the League respects the existing ruling system of the other member states in the League, and considers it a right of those states, and promises not to take any action aiming at changing that system.[3]

As soon as he reappeared in October 1962, Imam Muhammad al-Badr sent a telegram to the secretary-general of the League informing him that he was still alive and asking him to call for an immediate meeting of the Council.[4] In the meantime, the League received a similar request from the republican government in Sanaa.[5] Nevertheless, Abd al-Khaliq Hassouna, the League's secretary-general, influenced by President Nasser, failed to perform his responsibility in a constructive manner, ignored the Imam's request and instead recognized the republican regime in Sanaa as the legitimate government.[6] This "biased" position on the part of the League served to limit the effective role that it might have played in the Yemeni dilemma. In addition to this action, the Council also adopted Resolution 1911 on September 19, 1963, which asked member states to extend all help to the republican regime in Sanaa and to support it in the international arena.[7] This development confirmed the pointedly one-sided position of the League, as it opted to support but one Yemeni faction in the conflict, the republicans, while ignoring the second one, the royalists, who were suffering from the brutality of the Egyptian military operations against them.

Nevertheless, the same resolution entrusted the Council's chairman and the secretary-general to carry out the necessary contacts that would help promote the restoration of peace in Yemen and the resumption of normal relations among the disputing parties, namely, Saudi Arabia,

Egypt, Yemen and Jordan.[8] Despite the fact that this was viewed by many states as a positive move, one cannot ignore the reality that it came too late, particularly from a regional organization that was supposed to be the first to act.[9] However, a "peace mission" was formed in mid-September by the League and was authorized to visit the various countries concerned.

On September 25, 1963, the mission arrived in Taif, the summer capital of Saudi Arabia, where it met with Crown Prince Faisal, who informed the mission of his personal desire to avoid any kind of military clash between Saudi and Yemeni troops. Similarly, Saudi Arabia expressed its desire to cooperate fully in strengthening Arab solidarity and the restoration of normal relations among all Arab states. From there the League mission proceeded to Jordan where it met with King Hussein on October 1, 1963. King Hussein informed the mission that his country did not consider itself part of the conflict.[10] On October 6, 1963, the mission arrived in Sanaa. There it met with President Abdallah al-Sallal and then abruptly left for Egypt without meeting with either the Imam or his royalist supporters.[11] As stated to the author recently, the Imam characterized the role of the Arab League in the Yemeni crisis by saying that "it was on a vacation."[12]

The League, as personified in its "peace mission," actually ignored and disregarded both the existence and the right of the royalist forces to be consulted or, at least, given the chance to articulate their views. By doing so, the League predetermined the fate of its mediation efforts. This became obvious during the mission's meeting with the Egyptian foreign minister in Cairo, who told its members that his government was obliged by the "disengagement agreement" and hoped that all parties concerned would carry out their obligations as stated in that agreement.[13] This Egyptian stand, compounded by the mission's failure to meet with the royalist representatives, resulted in the termination of the League's efforts to mediate in the Yemen crisis. In retrospect, it is clear that the Arab League, like other regional and international organizations, became a victim of regional and international disputes. In an interview with H.E. Mahmoud Riad, His Excellency was asked the following:

> The Arab League, which Your Excellency has served as a secretary-general, conducted some efforts and played an ineffective role in attempting to solve the Yemeni problem. What are the reasons behind its failure?

His Excellency replied that:

> International, as well as Arab, organizations are always victims of international and regional disputes. They try to carry out their peaceful role.

However, they always face a number of obstacles. This is exactly what happened to the Arab League throughout the Yemen crisis. Also, we have to take into consideration two major elements: (1) the personality of the secretary-general himself and his ability to use his powers and the facilities that are rendered to him; and (2) the role of the concerned parties, who really have control over the direction of events and political matters. From this we may come to the conclusion that the role of the Arab League in the Yemen problem was not decisive and fruitful because the right person was not available. In the meantime, Egypt and Saudi Arabia themselves were not helpful to the League and its efforts. Here we must recognize a fact and that is that Saudi Arabia and Egypt are the two Arab countries with the most political weight in the Arab world. This is what political events have proved and still prove day after day.[14]

Mr. Riad's analysis of the Arab League's capabilities and handicaps retains substantial validity. However, one may take issue with his view that Saudi Arabia was less than helpful to the League's efforts. In fact, as soon as the League's "peace mission" concluded its talks with Crown Prince Faisal in Taif, the Saudi government issued an official "joint communiqué" welcoming all attempts aimed at strengthening Arab solidarity and the restoration of normal relations among all Arab states.[15] It also expressed its desire to cooperate fully in achieving that goal. Nevertheless, Mr. Riad's view seems more appropriate in Egypt's case, which contributed to terminating the League's effort by referring "directly" to the "disengagement agreement" reached by the United States and supervised by the United Nations observation mission. By doing so, Egypt had made it clear to the "peace mission" that it did not need the League's efforts.

Between 1964 and 1967, the Arab Summit Conference played a constructive role in the Yemeni dilemma by urging all concerned parties in the conflict, as well as other Arab states, to continue efforts aimed at finding a suitable solution for the Yemeni dilemma.[16] The principal role and mediatory efforts of the League were conducted as part of other Arab states' initiatives and by offering its good offices to all parties concerned, with the exception of the royalist forces.

The U.N. Mediation Efforts

The United Nations was involved in the Yemen crisis on two levels. First, it conducted a mediation effort through Ambassador Ralph Bunche, U.N. undersecretary-general for political affairs, which unfortunately failed to produce fruitful results. Second, it undertook an observation mission which stemmed from the disengagement agreement engineered by U.S. Ambassador Ellsworth Bunker between Saudi Arabia and Egypt.

This mission did ameliorate the situation for some time but it failed to end the war.

The U.N. Mediatory Role

The United Nations mediatory role in Yemen began during the early months of 1963 with an American proposal to appoint Italian Ambassador Pier Pasquale Spinally as U.N. representative to the Middle East who, under the aegis of Secretary-General U Thant,[17] would attempt to find a solution to the Yemen conflict. However, as noted earlier, that proposal was turned down by the secretary-general. In the meantime, U Thant was reluctant to act without the explicit consent of all parties concerned with the Yemen crisis, namely, Saudi Arabia, Egypt and Yemen.

Nevertheless, by late fall 1962, the secretary-general began to consult U.N. representatives of the concerned parties, who expressed sympathetic and cooperative attitudes for a U.N. role in the conflict. This prompted the secretary-general's decision to send a "fact-finding" mission headed by Ralph Bunche to the area in late February-early March 1963, for the purpose of ascertaining the views of concerned parties on the situation.[18] However, the mission was less than a success. Crown Prince Faisal refused to see Bunche on the grounds that Bunche was not entirely neutral since he had visited Sanaa and Cairo but had failed to meet with the Yemeni royalists.[19] Another reason for Bunche's unsuccessful mission is that his mandate was limited to "fact-finding," and he was not authorized to negotiate a disengagement plan.[20]

In the meantime, the U.S. State Department notified the U.N. secretary-general of the mediatory efforts begun by Ambassador Ellsworth Bunker in early March 1963. Theoretically, Bunker's efforts were in support of Bunche's mission.[21] But Ambassador Bunker could not persuade Crown Prince Faisal to see Ambassador Bunche. The Crown Prince held to his position that if Bunche were not going to visit the royalists, he could not assume the proper posture of intermediary between Yemen and Saudi Arabia. Faisal added that this situation would put Saudi Arabia in the position of appearing to interfere in Yemeni domestic affairs; moreover, the quarrel was not between Yemen and Saudi Arabia—as Saudi Arabia had no relations with the Yemen Arab Republic and recognized the Imam instead—but rather was between Cairo and Saudi Arabia.[22] If Bunche were to attempt to mediate between Saudi Arabia and Egypt, Faisal added, he would find such efforts acceptable.

Thus Ambassador Bunche returned to U.N. headquarters without seeing Crown Prince Faisal. At the same time, he reported to the secretary-general that President Nasser of Egypt wanted only an assurance from Saudi Arabia that it would end its aid to the royalists. Bunche also reported that President al-Sallal of Yemen desired not only this assurance but also the expulsion of the ex-Imam and his family from Saudi Arabia, as well as Saudi and British recognition of his government. In return, he would refrain from intervening in Saudi Arabia and Aden.[23]

In the meantime, Ambassador Bunker returned to the United States on March 10, 1963, and urged the U.N. secretary-general to dispatch Ambassador Bunche to Saudi Arabia again to keep the mediation effort alive and to deter President Nasser from resuming his air raids on Saudi territories. U Thant insisted on two conditions for doing so:

1. That the Saudi representative to the United Nations should make clear that Crown Prince Faisal was going to receive Ambassador Bunche without requiring that he also visit the Yemeni royalists, and

2. That reactions be obtained from Cairo and Sanaa to the U.S. disengagement proposal.[24]

Since neither condition was met, the U.N. secretary-general decided not to send Ambassador Bunche to the Mideast as a mediator. Another reason for not sending him, according to the secretary-general, was that it probably would have required a resolution of the U.N. Security Council, which would have meant another delay. This, however, did not discourage the United States from continuing its mediation efforts, which have been characterized as being "in support of and ancillary to the U.N. efforts."[25] Nevertheless, the situation was so tense and delicate that the United States wanted full-time participation of the United Nations despite the reluctance of the secretary-general.

By April 10, 1963, Ambassador Bunker succeeded in achieving a "disengagement agreement" between Saudi Arabia and Egypt, requiring a U.N. observation mission to employ the disengagement terms. Upon his return to the United States on April 12, 1963, Ambassador Bunker requested that the secretary-general send a special representative to the Middle East to start discussions on the proper processes for carrying out the provisions of the disengagement agreement. Consequently, in late May 1963, U Thant sent Major General Carl Von Horn on an exploratory visit to Yemen, in preparation for the establishment of a U.N. Yemen Observation Mission.[26]

The U.N. Observer Role

The U.N. role as an observer partner in the Yemen crisis derived from the success which U.S. efforts produced in reaching an agreement between Saudi Arabia and Egypt, the major external parties in the Yemen crisis. Although this agreement was acceptable to the U.N. secretary-general, certain legal actions had to be taken according to

U.N. rules and regulations. First, a resolution needed to be passed in the Security Council to authorize the secretary-general to send the Yemen Observation Mission. Second, it was necessary to estimate the financial requirements for the mission and to establish who was going to finance it. Third, the duration of the mission, the number of troops and the amount of equipment required all had to be decided upon. Fourth, the task of the mission had to be precisely defined.

These legal actions, and the first in particular, required more time than the critical situation in Yemen permitted. The factor of urgency prompted the secretary-general to ask Major Carl Von Horn, chief of staff of the U.N. Truce Supervision Organization in Jerusalem, to proceed without delay to the three countries (Saudi Arabia, Egypt and Yemen) for consultations with the appropriate authorities on details relating to the nature and function of U.N. observers for implementation of the terms of the disengagement agreement. After completing his mission, Major General Van Horn reported to the secretary-general that he had talked with the three governments concerned and obtained their views on the role, functions, scope and strength of the proposed observation operation. All three parties, he added, confirmed their acceptance of identical terms of disengagement in Yemen. His conclusion was that United Nations observers at the Saudi-Yemeni borders were "vitally necessary and could well be the decisive factor in avoiding serious trouble in that area, and their presence is desired by all parties concerned."[27] As the need for these observers was urgent, they should be dispatched with the least possible delay, he added.

The secretary-general reported Horn's findings and recommendations to the Security Council on May 27, 1963, and proposed that a peace-keeping operation in Yemen, with a 200-man observer group, be established. Furthermore, due to the urgency of the situation, a small advance party should be sent to the area "within a few days." The observation mission would serve for no more than four months; a 100-man ground patrol unit would be armed only for self-defense. Some of the members of this mission could be recruited from the United Nations Emergency Force in the Middle East (UNEF), the United Nations' Truce Supervision Organization in Palestine (UNTSO) and possibly the United Nations' Military Observer Group in India and Pakistan (UNMOGIP). The total cost of the mission was estimated at less than $1 million, for which the secretary-general expressed the hope that the governments of Saudi Arabia and Egypt would bear at least part, with the balance, if necessary, being met by the United Nations.[28] This proposal led to the drafting of a resolution, submitted jointly by Ghana and Morocco, which aimed at defining precisely how to make the U.N. action legal and allow the organization to assume responsibility in a conflict which threatened international peace and security.[29]

Thus, on July 4, 1963, the U.N. observer team began its operation on the Saudi-Yemeni border in line with the Security Council decision. The team consisted of:

- 114 reconnaissance personnel, with Yugoslavian officers and other ranks;
- 50 airlift personnel, provided by Royal Canadian Air Force officers and other ranks, using Caribou and other aircraft and H-19 helicopters;
- 28 civilian staff from various countries; and
- 20 locally recruited employees to be based in Sanaa.[30]

Nevertheless, the mission's task and functions were limited to observing, certifying and reporting the withdrawal of troops, meaning that the operation had no broader peace-keeping role. Therefore, the mission could not effectively undertake any border functions with the personnel, equipment and funds available to it. In addition, the mission was not to be concerned with Yemen's internal affairs, with the actions of its government or with that government's relations with other governments and with bordering territories, nor did it have authority to issue orders or directions.

On September 4, 1963, the mission's mandate expired, and the U.N. secretary-general proposed an additional two months of observation, which was accepted by the Security Council as well as Egypt and Saudi Arabia. Extensions of the mission's mandate continued until September 1964, when the Saudi government announced that the Egyptians were not in compliance with the terms of the disengagement and therefore refused to agree to another extension.[31] The Saudi position was reaffirmed in a report of the secretary-general to the Security Council on the functioning of the U.N. Yemen Observation Mission (UNYOM) and the implementation of the terms of disengagement covering the period from January 3 to March 3, 1964. It reported that:

As regards to the strength of the United Arab Republic force in Yemen, the United Nations observers at Hodeida have reported that more than 4,000 UAR troops arrived there by sea from January 3 to February 18 while more than a thousand departed. The majority of these arriving troops seemed to be composed of organized military formation with appropriate equipment and transport, but a considerable number apparently consisted of individual soldiers returning from leave. It is customary for the UAR command to send troops from Yemen on leave in military transport aircraft which have brought supplies to their forces. While an exact determination of the number of troops involved is not possible, it is estimated that more than a thousand troops left by plane. Thus the effective strength of the UAR forces in Yemen during the period appears to have increased by some one to two thousand.[32]

Upon consulting the U.A.R. representative at the United Nations about the Saudi position and the intention of terminating the mission, the secretary-general was informed that the U.A.R. government had no objection to the mission's termination. Thus, arrangements were taken by the U.N. commander in Yemen to end his mission without accomplishing any solid success, save for limited progress towards implementation of the disengagement agreement. However, the U.N. failure should not be attributed only to the ineffectiveness of its mission in Yemen but to other factors as well. Among these were the constraints imposed on the mission's functions by the disengagement agreement, the dearth of financial support, the paucity of observers and the lack of cooperation by the parties concerned, particularly Egypt and Yemen.

Finally, one thing must be said about the role of regional and international organizations. Most of the problems with which they deal are virtually unsolvable before they ever reach these organizations. Mediation by international organizations is generally accepted as a last resort, after the parties directly concerned are unable to solve the dispute themselves. Bringing a dispute before the United Nations or a regional organization often means only that the disputants have another forum in which to air their charges. Mediation by international organizations can succeed only if all parties genuinely seek a mutually acceptable solution. This was not the case in Yemen.

Arab States' Mediation Efforts

While both Saudi Arabia and Egypt realized through the Yemeni crisis the danger of the situation and tried to solve the problem in their own way, other Arab states also attempted to mediate in the conflict and search for a solution. For example, Kuwait and Sudan, due to their proximity to the two major parties of the conflict (i.e., Saudi Arabia and Egypt), played the role of mediators. Algeria, Iraq and Jordan also contributed in this manner.

The Saudi-Egyptian Efforts

The first Saudi-Egyptian efforts to find a solution for the Yemeni crisis occurred in February 1964 when two representatives from Iraq and Algeria arrived in Riyadh, Saudi Arabia. There, in a number of meetings with Crown Prince Faisal, they offered to mediate between Saudi Arabia and Egypt.[33] The crown prince appreciated their concern and accepted their role, as well as the intended arrival of an Egyptian delegation to discuss the Yemeni conflict. Consequently, in March 1964 a U.A.R. mission headed by Vice President Abd al-Hakim Amir visited Riyadh and held talks with Crown Prince Faisal. The visit resulted in the resumption of diplomatic relations between the two countries and their declaration in favor of the absolute independence of Yemen.[34]

The second attempt by the same two states materialized during the second Arab summit in September 1964 in Alexandria, Egypt, when both President Nasser and Crown Prince Faisal met for the first time to discuss the Yemeni crisis face to face. At the end of their talks, the two leaders agreed to "fully cooperate in mediation with the concerned parties, i.e., royalist and republican Yemenis, in order to reach a peaceful solution of all problems in Yemen, and to continue these efforts until conditions stabilized there."[35] As a result of this Saudi-Egyptian agreement, representatives of Yemeni royalists and republicans met in Erkwit, Sudan, on October 30, 1964. There they agreed that a cease-fire would come into force on November 5, and a national congress, attended by representatives of both sides, would be held on November 23 of the same year. However, although the cease-fire came into effect, the congress never took place due to differences between the two Yemeni factions; by early December, fighting in Yemen had broken out once again.[36]

Mahmoud Riad is of the opinion that the Yemenis themselves were the principal reason for the failure of all agreements and peaceful mediation efforts. He believes that they took advantage of the situation by accepting financial support from both Saudi Arabia and Egypt and thus an end to the war was not in the economic interest of those opportunistic Yemenis.[37] Whereas some evidence exists to support Mr. Riad's opinion, the primary reason that the national congress never convened appeared to be the loss of interest by both the Egyptians and republicans in carrying out the Erkwit agreement.[38] At the same time, a division occurred among the republicans themselves over the deepening influence of the Egyptians on the government of North Yemen. That division resulted in the resignation of several prominent ministers who created the so-called "Third Force" and engaged in talks with the royalists.[39]

Nevertheless, a further deterioration of the Yemen crisis in June 1965 encouraged King Hussein of Jordan to send letters to President Nasser and King Faisal proposing a joint republican and royalist administration to rule Yemen until a general referendum could be held in the country to determine its future government. Meanwhile, U.A.R. troops could be replaced by an inter-Arab peace force.[40] In the interim, Algeria, acting alone this time, attempted to renew its mediation efforts by proposing that consultations be held on the problem in Sanaa, Cairo and Baghdad. Once again, these efforts failed to gain acceptance since neither Egypt nor the republican regime in Yemen was willing to compromise with the royalists.

Nevertheless, on August 22, 1965, President Nasser arrived in Jeddah, Saudi Arabia, where he personally held talks with King Faisal on the Yemeni dilemma.[41] Significantly, Nasser took this step after receiving several negative reports about the Egyptian troops in Yemen which indicated that:

1. Egyptian soldiers were unwilling to fight in Yemen;
2. Egyptian troops were not likely to keep up morale in a country and society so different from their own and so little to their liking; and
3. The Yemeni revolutionaries were in disagreement on the role and function of the Egyptians in Yemen.[42]

The two leaders, nonetheless, agreed on another cease-fire date and signed the well-known Jeddah agreement on August 24, 1965. This accord provided for:

1. An immediate cease-fire and the formation by Saudi Arabia and the United Arab Republic of a joint peace commission to supervise the cease-fire and control the frontiers and ports; a joint force of the two countries would be set up, to be used by the commission in order to prevent any violation of the agreement or any action intended to obstruct it or provoke disorder;
2. The immediate ending of Saudi Arabian military aid to the royalists and the prevention of the use of its territory for operations against Yemen;
3. The withdrawal of all United Arab Republic forces from Yemen within ten months beginning from November 23, 1965;
4. The holding of a plebiscite not later than November 23, 1966, through which the people of Yemen would decide which form of government they desired; and
5. A conference of all national forces and leading personalities of Yemen, to be held at Harad on November 23, 1965, to decide the system of government during the transitional period up to the plebiscite, form a provisional government and determine the form and nature of the plebiscite.[43]

The Jeddah agreement succeeded partially in cooling down the situation in Yemen. The Harad conference, too, was held on time in accordance with the Jeddah agreement, and both Saudi and Egyptian representatives attended it. However, after three promising days of negotiations, the conference fell into a "deadlock" on the issue of the name to be given to the new state. This stemmed from a disagreement among the parties as to whether the Jeddah Agreement intended to abolish the Imamate or establish a republic—a point which the agreement did not address.[44] Another reason for the "deadlock" was that Egypt lost interest in the Jeddah agreement, just as it had before with regard to the Erkwit talks.[45]

The Egyptian command in Sanaa sent a warning to Qadi Abd al-Rahman al-Iryani, the head of the republican delegation to the Harad negotiations, threatening that he and his colleagues would be "buried alive" if they agreed to accept the principle of "self-determination" or agreed to drop the use of the word "republic" to describe the transitional regime.[46] Subsequently, the conference recessed on December 24, 1965, without making any substantial progress. By early 1966, President Nasser introduced his so-called "Long Breath Strategy" which resulted in increasing Egypt's involvement in Yemen.

The Kuwaiti and Sudanese Efforts

Although the Kuwaitis began their mediation efforts as early as June 1965, i.e., about 18 months before the Sudanese, both countries' plans were basically similar. They both stressed the need for withdrawal of Egyptian troops and of the Imam's family, the presence of an inter-Arab peace-keeping force of 3,000 men and a plebiscite to be conducted by representatives of "neutral Arab states."[47]

In June 1965, a mediation mission headed by the crown prince of Kuwait visited Riyadh and discussed the Yemeni crisis with King Faisal, who afterwards accepted Kuwait's mediatory role. However, the Kuwaitis halted their efforts in the wake of President Nasser's visit to Saudi Arabia in August of the same year and the subsequent signing of the Jeddah agreement. With the collapse of the Jeddah agreement, Kuwait resumed its mediation efforts in mid-May 1966, with Shaykh Sabah al-Ahmad al-Sabah, the Kuwait foreign minister, conducting "shuttle-diplomacy" between Riyadh and Cairo. On May 20, 1966, Kuwait proposed that the personal representative of President Nasser, Sayyid Hasan Sabri al-Khuli, along with Shaykh Sabah al-Ahmad, should visit Saudi Arabia to discuss the Yemen question with King Faisal. The proposal was immediately rejected by Egypt under the pretext that "no benefit was likely to result from such a proposal."[48]

This notwithstanding, Sayyid al-Khuli did visit Kuwait on May 30, where he had discussions with Shaykh Sabah al-Ahmad about Yemen, but both agreed not to publish anything about their talks.[49] On June

12, 1966, Shaykh Sabah al-Ahmad stopped in Saudi Arabia with a message from the Kuwait amir to King Faisal and then went on to Cairo where he met with President Nasser. This kind of shuttle-diplomacy continued until August 2, 1966, when Shaykh Sabah reported to the Kuwaiti Cabinet that both King Faisal and President Nasser had agreed to their representatives' meeting in Kuwait to discuss the Kuwaiti proposals.[50] However, the meeting never took place, and the Kuwaitis ultimately suspended their mediation efforts.

The Sudanese mediation efforts, on the other hand, began in early December 1966 during the visit to Saudi Arabia of Sayyid Ismail al-Azhari, president of the Sudanese Supreme Council. During his visit, President al-Azhari offered Sudanese mediation in the Yemen dispute and was encouraged by King Faisal's positive response. Thus, the Sudanese began a shuttle-diplomacy similar to that of the Kuwaitis.

The June 1967 Arab-Israeli war broke out while the Sudanese mediation effort was underway, forcing Egypt to reconsider its role in Yemen. This new atmosphere enabled the Sudanese prime minister, Muhammad Ahmad Mahjub, to achieve a successful end to the Sudanese mediation effort. On August 20, 1967, just prior to the Arab summit meeting in Khartoum, Mahjub visited Saudi Arabia where he met with King Faisal and drew up a new peace plan. The plan remained secret until he discussed it with President Nasser in Cairo on August 24, 1967.[51]

On August 29, 1967, the Arab summit convened in Khartoum with both King Faisal and President Nasser in attendance. The following day, Nasser suggested to Premier Mahjub that he and King Faisal meet in Mahjub's house to discuss the "Yemen Peace Plan." The meeting took place as planned, and both parties agreed on settling the Yemen problem. The text of the agreement as broadcast by Radio Cairo was as follows:

> In eagerness to clear the Arab atmosphere; in order to strengthen the ties of friendship and brotherhood among the Arab people; and in order to settle the problem of Yemen, agreement has been reached on the following:
>
> 1. Formation of a committee of three which will be entrusted with dealing with the problem. The committee shall be formed by Saudi Arabia choosing one Arab state, the UAR a second Arab state and third state to be chosen by the foreign ministers of Arab states or by mutual agreement of both parties.
>
> 2. The committee's mission is to work out plans which would guarantee withdrawal of UAR forces in Yemen and stop military assistance extended by Saudi Arabia to Yemenis.
>
> 3. The committee shall exert its efforts in order to enable the Yemenis to unite, live in harmony and achieve stability in accord with the true

desire of the people of the country and in recognition of Yemen's right to full independence and sovereignty.

4. The committee will consult with the Kingdom of Saudi Arabia and UAR on all problems hampering its progress, with the aim of solving them and reaching an understanding acceptable to the parties concerned so that the cause of this dispute can be removed, Arab blood saved, Arab ranks consolidated, and so that good will prevail.[52]

Iraq, Morocco and Sudan were chosen to constitute the committee proposed in the agreement.

In summary, the Egyptian-Saudi agreement turned on several factors. First, the 1967 Arab defeat put an end to Nasser's Pan-Arab ambitions. Second, the deterioration of the Egyptian economy precluded any further support for the Yemeni republicans. Third, most prominent republicans, apart from pro-Egyptians like al-Sallal and Guzaylan, were in favor of reconciliation with the royalist forces. Fourth, Saudi Arabia was willing to tolerate a Yemeni republic with royalist participation. Fifth and finally, both Egypt and Saudi Arabia desired to end Arab bloodshed in the aftermath of the June 1967 debacle.

Despite the agreement, the Yemeni dilemma did not end immediately and the civil war dragged on for more than three years. This was a result of Yemeni President al-Sallal's rejection of the agreement on grounds that Yemen was not a party to it, and his subsequent refusal to meet with the peace committee in Sanaa.[53] Consequently, the situation remained tense in Yemen despite Egypt's withdrawal and the cessation of Saudi Arabia's aid to the royalists. The tripartite committee, comprised of Iraq, Morocco and Sudan, carried out its peace efforts to no avail. But finally, in 1970, peace was achieved, largely through Saudi mediation efforts between the royalists and the republicans.

The Saudi Efforts After 1967

Following Egypt's withdrawal from Yemen in 1967, the civil war degenerated into stalemate. The ex-Imam and his supporters continued to fight against the republicans but failed to reconquer Sanaa, the capital, despite some success in capturing and occupying a number of major Yemeni cities and towns.[54]

Abdallah al-Sallal was overthrown on November 5, 1967, while on a visit to Iraq. A new, moderate government emerged under the leadership of Qadi Abd al-Rahman al-Iryani. Unlike al-Sallal, the new Yemeni leadership was willing to accept the terms of the Khartoum agreement between Saudi Arabia and Egypt. The new Y.A.R. leadership also accepted, under the banner of "national reconciliation," the participation of some Yemeni royalists in the republican government.[55] In addition, the new government was ready to talk to the tripartite Arab committee, which had been agreed upon in accordance with the Khartoum agreement. These developments were one factor in the changing Yemen political scene which, by early 1969, opened the way for constructive and meaningful negotiations between the two Yemeni factions.

Moreover, two decisive events took place in March 1969, which led to the disintegration of resistance by the Hamid al-Din royal family. First, Prince Muhammad ibn al-Husayn resigned as the Imam's deputy, and he abandoned the cause.[56] Prince Muhammad's resignation resulted from widespread royalist opposition to his continued insistence on offensive operations and his opposition to negotiations. Second, the Imam, believing that no positive results could come of continued fighting, decided to give his followers the freedom to decide their own fate, as well as that of Yemen as a whole.[57] This decision automatically absolved the royalists of their allegiance to both the Imam personally and the Hamid al-Din family in general.

As a consequence, by early 1970, the conviction was widespread that reconciliation between Yemeni republicans and royalists had become a necessity. King Faisal then met with representatives of the Yemeni royalists and encouraged them to negotiate with the republican prime minister to discuss a reconciliation agreement. The Islamic Conference of Foreign Ministers, which met in Jeddah from March 23–26, 1970, and which was attended by a Yemeni republican delegation led by the prime minister, provided the opportunity for such a meeting. After the end of the conference, both republican and royalist Yemeni factions began their negotiations with Saudi Arabia, which served as host as well as an observer.

Reconciliation depended upon the satisfactory resolution of two specific issues, namely, the future name of Yemen and the role of the royal family. The republicans insisted on a *jumhuriya* (republic), while the royalists pressed for the designation of *dawla* (state). The issue was resolved, with Saudi concurrence, when the Yemeni royalists accepted President Nasser's appeal to retain the name of the republic. The second issue was resolved when the Imam granted his permission to his followers to make their own decisions, a step which automatically freed them of allegiance to him and his family.[58]

Negotiations between the royalists and the republicans succeeded in May 1970 in reaching agreement on national reconciliation. This agreement allowed several of the royalists to join the Yemeni cabinet, among them Ahmad al-Shami, who served as a foreign minister in the royalists' government in exile. The May 1970 agreement was preceded by Saudi recognition of the Yemeni republican regime, on April 8, 1970,[59] which

demonstrated to both sides the Saudi position in favor of the reconciliation. By accepting the republican government, Saudi Arabia also
demonstrated that it had no desire to interfere in the domestic affairs
of its neighbors.

Thus, Saudi recognition of the republican regime in Yemen and the
reconciliation agreement reached by the royalists and republicans ended
eight years of bloody civil war in Yemen. Given this, one must accept
the fact that troubled nations possess the key to their problems' solutions,
and they are usually the only ones who can determine their future.
Nevertheless, while the end of the civil war ushered in a new era of
Yemen's history, it did not solve all of its national problems.

> The experience of Civil War eventually resulted in the creation of a new
> political culture or environment, albeit one without a logical or even
> contrived focus. Theoretically, national reconciliation had laid the foun-
> dation for a unified state to pursue the goals of political growth and socio-
> economic development. In actuality, progress on the fronts of development
> and political stability continued to be hampered by factionalism, rampant
> personal ambitions, infrastructural stagnation and the regime's basic lack
> of legitimacy.[60]

* * *

Since the end of the civil war in 1970, Saudi Arabia has continued
to view the Yemen state with acute interest. It soon becomes apparent
to anyone who has followed the Saudi involvement in that conflict that
Saudi Arabia considers Yemen's fate as integrally linked to its own. For
that reason, the next chapter will focus on the relationship which has
developed between Saudi Arabia and North Yemen since the end of
the civil war.

Notes

[1] Hussein A. Hassouna, *The League of Arab States and Regional Disputes:
A Study of Middle East Conflicts* (Dobbs Ferry, NY: Oceana; Leiden: A. W.
Sijthoff, 1975), p. 184.

[2] Ibrahim al-Shurayqi, *Al-Sira al-Dami fil-Yaman* [The Bloody Conflict in
Yemen], 1st ed. (n.p., August 1964), p. 51.

[3] Ibid., pp. 51–52.

[4] Hassouna, p. 184.

[5] Al-Shurayqi, p. 51.

[6] The Arab League Council accepted the credentials of the republican delegate
on March 23, 1963, during the Council's 38th ordinary session. Saudi Arabia
along with Jordan and several other states opposed the move.

[7] This resolution was adopted in response to Yemen's appeal to the Council for assistance and to intervene to put an end to the strained relations between Yemen and certain member states. In fact, the appeal was presented during the 40th ordinary session of the Council. Both Saudi Arabia and Jordan abstained.

[8] Butrus Butrus Ghali, *Al-Jamiah al-Arabiyah wa Taswiyat al-Munazat al-Mahalliyah* [The Arab League and the Resolution of Local Disputes] (Cairo: n.p., 1977), p. 117.

[9] The United Nations acted as early as February and March 1963, whereas the Arab League began to move as late as September 25, 1963, almost a year after the Yemeni crisis had begun.

[10] Ghali, pp. 117–118.

[11] Hassouna, p. 186.

[12] Interview with H.M. Imam Muhammad al-Badr, London: December 21, 1983. Appendix No. 2, Question and Answer Number 10.

[13] Hassouna, p. 186.

[14] Interview with H.E. Mahmoud Riad, Cairo: November 11, 1984. Appendix No. 4, Question and Answer Number 8.

[15] Ghali, p. 118.

[16] Hassouna, pp. 186–190.

[17] Christopher J. McMullen, *Resolution of the Yemen Crisis 1963, "A Case Study in Mediation"* (Washington, DC: Institute for the Study of Diplomacy, School of Foreign Service, Georgetown University), p. 7.

[18] Report of the Secretary-General to the Security Council concerning Developments Relating to Yemen, Document S/5298, April 29, 1963.

[19] McMullen, p. 10.

[20] *United Nations Review*, vol. 10, no. 3 (March 1963), p. 1.

[21] It is interesting to note that while the United States was considering its efforts as supportive to those of the United Nations, the secretary-general was insisting that the U.S. efforts were unconnected with those of the United Nations.

[22] McMullen, pp. 13–14.

[23] Ibid., p. 17.

[24] Ibid.

[25] Report of the Secretary-General to the Security Council Concerning Developments Relating to Yemen, Document S/5298, April 29, 1963.

[26] *United Nations Review*, vol. 10, no. 5 (May 1963), p. 1.

[27] *United Nations Review*, vol. 10, no. 6 (June 1963), pp. 1–2.

[28] *United Nations Review*, vol. 10, no. 7 (July 1963), p. 17.

[29] Ibid., p. 16. The vote on this resolution was ten in favor and none against, with one abstention, by the Soviet Union.

[30] *United Nations Review*, vol. 10, no. 9 (October 1963), p. 23.

[31] McMullen, p. 48.

[32] Secretary-General's Report, Document S/5572, March 3, 1964.

[33] The Iraqi-Algerian mediation efforts came about as a result of the first Arab summit held in Cairo in January 1964.

[34] Hassouna, p. 187.

35 Amin Said, *Tarikh al-Dawlah al-Saudiyah* [The History of the Saudi State], vol. 3 (Beirut: n.p., 1965), pp. 362–363. Also see Hassouna, pp. 187–188.

36 Ibid., p. 188. In fact, the congress did not take place because the republicans insisted that three-fifths of the representatives should be republicans, while the royalists wanted equal representation. At the same time, the two factions disagreed on the location of the congress.

37 Interview with H.E. Mahmoud Riad, Cairo: November 11, 1984. Appendix No. 4, Question and Answer Number 4.

38 Dana A. Schmidt, *Yemen: The Unknown War* (New York: Holt, Rinehart and Winston, 1968), p. 210.

39 *The Economist*, April 3, 1965, p. 34. Saudi Arabia supported these efforts but also arranged for a conference at Taif, Saudi Arabia, which was attended by 500 delegates from the royalists and republicans. However, nothing substantive came out of this meeting.

40 Hassouna, pp. 188–189.

41 Ibid., p. 189.

42 *Arab Report and Record*, May 16–31, 1965, p. 120.

43 Hassouna, p. 189.

44 The republicans interpreted the agreement provision referring to the name of the state as one that should be only applied after the plebiscite, meaning that the name "Yemen Arab Republic" would remain in effect until the plebiscite was completed. The royalists, on the other hand, interpreted that provision as meaning the abolition of the "republican" system during the transition period and its replacement by an alternative system neither republican nor royalist.

45 The main purpose of Nasser's visit to Saudi Arabia in 1965 and his signature on the Jeddah agreement was aimed at putting pressure on the Soviets to respond positively to his request for $200 million worth of aid and equipment to continue his involvement in Yemen. Therefore, once he signed the agreement, he informed the Soviets that unless he got what he needed he was going to withdraw from Yemen, a step that the Soviets did not want him to take. Consequently, they supplied him with what he had asked for, and that made him lose interest in the Jeddah agreement. A prominent Saudi official told the author of this incident.

46 "Yemen: The War and the Haradh Conference," *Review of Politics*, vol. 28, no. 3 (July 1966), pp. 321–325.

47 *Arab Report and Record*, May 16–31, 1966, p. 120.

48 Ibid.

49 A high-ranking Saudi official.

50 *Arab Report and Record*, August 1–15, 1966, p. 180.

51 Muhammad Ahmad Mahjub, *al-Dimuqratiyah fil-Mizan* [Democracy in the Balance] (Beirut: Dar al-Nahar, 1973), p. 163.

52 *Arab Report and Record*, August 16–31, 1967, p. 269.

53 Ibid., p. 283, and Ghali, p. 126.

54 The Kingdom of Saudi Arabia did not finance any of these post-1967 war efforts and adhered fully to the Khartoum agreement.

55 Abd al-Rahman al-Boyidani, *Azmat al-Umah al-Arabiyah wa Thawrat al-Yaman* [The Crisis of the Arab Nation and the Yemeni Revolution] (Cairo:

Matabi al-Maktab al-Misri al-Hadith, 1984), p. 749. The royalists who joined al-Iryanis government excluded members of the Hamid al-Din family, who were barred from residence in Yemen.

[56] A high-ranking Saudi official.

[57] Interview with H.M. Imam Muhammad al-Badr, London: December 21, 1983, Appendix No. 2, Question and Answer Number 14.

[58] After Prince Muhammad ibn al-Husayn's resignation, the Imam left for Jeddah, Saudi Arabia, and from there for Great Britain, where he still resides.

[59] *The New York Times*, April 10, 1970.

[60] J. E. Peterson, *Yemen: The Search for a Modern State* (Baltimore: The Johns Hopkins University Press, 1982), p. 172.

Chapter 7

SAUDI ARABIA AND NORTH YEMEN: THE INEVITABLE PARTNERSHIP

The Yemen war constituted a serious challenge to the Kingdom of Saudi Arabia, certainly from 1962 through 1967, and in some respects even up to 1970. The kingdom mobilized its military, political and economic assets in defense against the perceived expansionist policies and revolutionary assertions of President Nasser of Egypt. In fact, the kingdom met the challenge of Nasser and precluded his opportunity to dominate Yemen—a prize which Nasser was eager to secure as an initial foothold toward his goal of controlling the entire Arabian Peninsula.

The enduring lesson of Yemen's civil war for Saudi Arabia may be the demonstration of the kingdom's extreme vulnerability to events and developments in Yemen. Since the trauma of the 1960s, Saudi Arabia and Yemen have joined together in an inevitable partnership, from which neither side can comfortably extricate itself. A decade and a half after the end of the civil war, relations between the two countries appear as strong as they have ever been and give every promise of remaining closely intertwined far into the future. In addition to placing the Yemen crisis of the 1960s into the wider context of Arab politics during that period, this chapter seeks to clarify a point that has often puzzled observers of Saudi-Yemeni relations—how the kingdom perceives North Yemen and its place in Saudi security.

The Nature of the Saudi-Yemeni Relationship

North Yemen is of major importance to the Kingdom of Saudi Arabia, and indeed to the entire Arabian Peninsula. Maintaining peace, stability and deterring Soviet influence in North Yemen and the Arabian Peninsula has been and will remain a preeminent Saudi priority. In the meantime,

Saudi policy has aimed at narrowing the gap of mutual understanding between itself and North Yemen through pragmatic political policies and generous foreign aid programs. Toward this end, Saudi Arabia, in addition to supporting specific projects, provides general budgetary aid to the central government, estimated at $100–$400 million a year.[1] This kind of financial and economic support is channeled through a Yemeni-Saudi Coordinating Committee, headed by H.R.H. Prince Sultan ibn Abd al-Aziz, the Saudi defense minister. In fact, this committee was formed in July 1970 immediately after Saudi recognition of the republican government in Sanaa.[2] This policy so far has been moderately successful, and the kingdom likely will continue to pursue it to promote cooperation and, where possible, to insure peace and stability in the area.

The political system of a country is undoubtedly a major determinant in its foreign policy behavior. Accordingly, the more closely one country's political system resembles that of another, the greater is the degree of mutual understanding which can be expected between them. Conversely, as the differences between the political systems widen, so do their chances for misunderstanding. These premises have proved so valid over periods of time that they have been accepted by almost every political thinker of the twentieth century.

When comparing the political systems of Saudi Arabia and North Yemen, it is necessary to examine four factors which together have determined their respective political systems: domestic ideological orientation, internal security aspects, foreign policy orientation, and economic philosophy and policy orientation.

Domestic Ideological Orientation

Both Saudi Arabia and North Yemen recognize Islam as the official religion. In addition, Saudi Arabia is responsible for safeguarding the two holiest cities of Islam, Makkah and al-Madinah.

Since they are both Islamic states, Saudi Arabia and North Yemen recognize the *shariah*, or Islamic law, as the basis for their legal systems. Islamic law defines the rights, duties, obligations, and responsibilities of both ruler and ruled. In Saudi Arabia and North Yemen, religious leaders, who are also interpreters of the *shariah*, are respected. Furthermore, they play an important and, indeed, salient role in the government process.[3] The principal avenue of public expression and participation in the political process of Saudi Arabia is through the traditional Islamic means of consultation (*shura*) and consensus (*ijma*).[4] The principles also are present in North Yemen, where they have been formally incorporated into a Consultative Assembly.[5]

Similarities in domestic ideological orientation form the basis for a mutual understanding between the two countries. This is largely the result of a shared religion and the place it holds in the state, highly traditional societies, and conservative political systems.

Internal Security Aspects

Saudi Arabia, being a strong family-oriented and homogeneous society, has experienced few internal security problems involving Saudi nationals. The incidents of unrest which did occur involving Saudi nationals during the 1960s involved Shii Muslims in the Eastern Province.[6] Special government development programs for the Shii, aimed at resolving these problems, have largely alleviated them, particularly after the Shii demonstrations of 1979–1980.

In contrast to the situation existing with Saudi nationals, the hundreds of thousands of foreign nationals resident in Saudi Arabia have created a potential threat to internal security. There is little evidence, however, to suggest that any immediate threat currently exists or will arise in the foreseeable future. Moreover, the Saudi government is currently in the process of developing a modern police force equipped with the most advanced security equipment and manned by competent, educated, and experienced personnel.[7] Should any potential threat arise, Saudi Arabia is capable both of detecting it and dealing with it.

North Yemen, in contrast, has numerous internal security problems and a far-less-developed internal security force to deal with them. Its greatest internal security problems include the challenge to the central government's authority in rural areas, the problem of creating a national identity in a basically tribal society, the existence of Islamic sectarian rivalry, and the continuing possibility of insurgents infiltrating from South Yemen.[8]

The central government has attempted a number of strategies to deal with these problems. In asserting its authority over rural areas, by building hospitals and schools and by offering other public services in these areas, North Yemen has tried to convince its people that cooperation with the central government will bring prosperity and enhance their future prospects. Financial and security constraints have slowed this approach, and the government has experienced only modest success in achieving its goals.[9]

National integration in Yemen has been a major priority since the end of the civil war in 1970. In this regard, the central government has tried to encourage a common sense of identity which supersedes tribal and sectarian affiliation, personal loyalties and political preferences.[10] The absence of continuity in leadership, financial constraints and external pressures has seriously hampered these efforts.

Sectarian rivalry between Shii Zaydis in the northern part of the Yemen Arab Republic and Sunni Shafiis in the southern part of the country and in the neighboring People's Democratic Republic of Yemen (P.D.R.Y.) indicates the major political, religious and security problem that has existed for centuries. The problem is aggravated by the infiltration of South Yemen-backed insurgents, largely Shafii, across the border into North Yemen, where they maintain hostilities in the southern Y.A.R. that carry tribal as well as sectarian overtones. The North Yemeni central government has attempted to neutralize the insurgency by calling for unity between the two Yemens. To date, this approach has met with only limited success. However, an army campaign in 1982 drove the rebels out of virtually all Y.A.R. territory.

The widely divergent internal security situations existing in Saudi Arabia and North Yemen have fostered a relatively low level of understanding between them. The internal security problems of North Yemen make it difficult for Saudi Arabia to deal with North Yemen and its fragmented society. Despite this difficulty, Saudi Arabia has remained flexible in its relations with North Yemen.

Economic Philosophy and Policy Orientation

North Yemen, with per capita income approximating $320 per year, is among the poorest countries in the Arab world. Although North Yemenis working in Saudi Arabia and other Gulf states have sent home large portions of their earnings in the form of remittances, these payments have not, by and large, been used to develop the domestic economy. In contrast to the economic situation existing in North Yemen, Saudi Arabia is one of the richest countries in the world, with a per capita income of $11,160 per year.[11]

Both Saudi Arabia and North Yemen have adopted capitalist economic systems; both have also instituted open door economic policies. In both cases, these systems and policies have spurred further economic development. Furthermore, in pursuing these economic paths, North Yemen has taken advantage of the oil wealth which has benefited the entire Arabian Peninsula in the last fifteen years.[12]

Saudi Arabia and North Yemen both stressed social, economic and educational development. These two countries have become intertwined economically for several reasons. First, the labor remittances sent home by the 500,000 Yemenis working in Saudi Arabia in the early 1980s fueled domestic Yemeni demand for imported foodstuffs, luxury items and other consumer goods. Many of these goods were smuggled into Yemen from Saudi Arabia. Second, Saudi Arabia has underwritten a substantial portion of the Y.A.R. government's regular budget and military expenses since the end of the civil war. Third, Riyadh has also been generous in providing financial assistance for a number of development projects in Yemen, thereby stimulating economic demand in Yemen. These factors, coupled with the other similarities in their economic policy orientation, have facilitated a mutual understanding of domestic economic issues facing them.

Foreign Policy Orientation

Since the state's creation by the late King Abd al-Aziz in 1932, Saudi Arabia's foreign policy has sought to preserve its Islamic way of life and that of the entire Muslim world. The kingdom, as the guardian of the Muslim holy places of Makkah and al-Madinah, feels a special responsibility for preserving Islamic values and ways. In pursuing this objective, Saudi Arabia has established close relations with the Islamic world. In the meantime, it pursued steady and clear relations with the West, particularly the United States. Although North Yemen's foreign policy is also Islamic and often Western oriented, the Yemen Arab Republic, in an attempt to play East off against West to its own advantage, also seeks to maintain good relations with Moscow and Eastern-bloc countries.[13]

While Saudi Arabia's foreign policy has been highly consistent, the hallmark of North Yemen's foreign policy has been its gross inconsistency. Frequent and often violent government changes in North Yemen have left the country without a well-known and well-defined foreign policy.[14] At the same time, North Yemen's attempt to play East off against West has created difficulties in its relations both with Saudi Arabia and with the United States.[15]

Both Saudi Arabia and North Yemen support Palestinian rights, while advocating a peaceful and just solution to the Arab-Israeli dilemma.[16] In addition, both countries have consistently supported Islamic countries in Asia and Africa. Despite these similarities, it appears that the differences in the foreign-policy orientation of Saudi Arabia and North Yemen constitute a major obstacle on the level of understanding between them. It is quite possible, however, that in the future the similarities between them could serve to draw the two closer together.

After reviewing the domestic ideological orientation, internal security aspects, foreign policy orientation, and economic philosophy and policy orientation of Saudi Arabia and North Yemen, one is left with the conviction that these countries will reach a high level of mutual understanding only if their political systems become more closely aligned. Such a development undoubtedly would enhance the degree of bilateral relations and understanding between them. These same factors—ideology, internal security, foreign policy and economic policy—are also important to an understanding of the Saudi perception of North Yemen.

Saudi Perception of North Yemen

Saudi Arabia views Yemen from three different perspectives: the political, security and strategic standpoints. From the political perspective, Saudi policymakers, when considering North Yemen, focus on its political importance to the Arabian Peninsula as a whole. In considering North Yemen from the security angle, Saudis are concerned with how the internal security of Saudi Arabia could be affected by developments in North Yemen. Finally, considered strategically, Saudi policymakers are concerned with how and where North Yemen fits into the regional and international policies of Saudi Arabia.

In the aftermath of the 1967 Arab-Israeli war, Saudi Arabia began to assert a more active role in Arab politics. Given its vast oil reserves and the petrodollar influence it was therefore able to wield, Saudi Arabia soon assumed a leadership position among the moderate Arab states. Saudi Arabia's foreign policy since 1970 has been based on three major objectives: to prevent the spread of Soviet influence in the Middle East; to insure political stability and continuation of "moderate" regimes in the region; and to find a solution to the Arab-Israeli conflict that is acceptable to all parties concerned.[17] Given these foreign policy objectives and the premises underlying them, the kingdom has been alarmed both by the actual Soviet military presence in South Yemen after 1967 (following the British withdrawal from Aden Protectorates) and the potential Soviet presence in North Yemen. Viewing either the actual or potential presence of the Soviet Union in the region as a major threat to the area's stability, Saudi Arabia has labored hard diplomatically to prevent North Yemen from falling into the Soviet orbit. As a matter of course, Saudi Arabia's perception of North Yemen and its policy toward it have been greatly conditioned by its view of the Soviet threat.

Political Perceptions

The paramount considerations in Saudi Arabia's view of North Yemen's political importance turn on geopolitics and manpower. North Yemen's geopolitical significance is derived in great part from its location, which commands the strait of Bab al-Mandab. Freedom of navigation through this strait holds critical importance to Saudi Arabia primarily because this waterway is used extensively to transport oil from the Arabian Gulf to Europe. North Yemen's proximity to the kingdom and to the other Gulf oil-producing states is another salient geopolitical factor. Further, North Yemeni manpower represents a significant source of unskilled and semi-skilled labor in Saudi Arabia in particular and the Gulf area in general.[18] Both geopolitical and manpower factors make North Yemen's political allegiance and friendship vital to the success of Saudi political goals, especially within the Arabian Peninsula.

Since the early 1950s, Saudi Arabia has looked upon North Yemen as a country which—depending on its own fortunes—could act either as a stabilizing or a destabilizing force in the Arabian Peninsula.[19] Moreover, Saudi concern over which of these roles Yemen might play was reinforced by developments in the Peninsula. Foremost among these relevant developments have been persistent Soviet efforts to infiltrate North Yemen, historical tensions in the Gulf such as the Iraqi-Kuwaiti conflict, and internal strife in Bahrain. All these concerns have strengthened the Saudi penchant for stability.

With regard to political development, Saudi Arabia regards North Yemen as a country that has suffered from traditional, repressive and colonialist regimes and from a more modern oppressor, the so-called revolutionary regime.[20] Yemen's dependence on foreign aid, because of its scarcity of natural resources other than manpower,[21] contributes to the problems of its government. Seeing its economic and governmental woes, Saudi Arabia, as a rich and politically stable country, has contributed significantly to the economic development of North Yemen. Saudi Arabia sees this as a means of promoting political stability in that country.

Saudi Arabia also watches the regional foreign policies of North Yemen with interest because of their effect on the Arabian Peninsula and the Gulf. For instance, Saudi Arabia is keenly interested in how North Yemen approaches the issues of Red Sea security and the granting of military privileges to the Soviet Union. In great part because of Saudi efforts and influence, North Yemen has refrained from allowing substantial Soviet political and military penetration.[22]

As Saudi Arabia sees it, continuing political instability in North Yemen constitutes yet another factor threatening the stability of the entire Arabian Peninsula. Saudi Arabia finds support for this view in the insurgency South Yemen supported in North Yemen throughout the 1970s. Actions such as these have exacerbated Saudi fears of communist "encirclement" and of regional unrest. Saudi Arabia viewed the insurgency in North Yemen during the 1970s as a Soviet tactic aimed at further enhancing its presence in the area and at exercising greater strength in the Arabian Peninsula.

Despite its suspicion of the Soviets, Saudi Arabia also understands that the internal situation in North Yemen requires that limited relations be maintained with the Soviet Union. Moreover, Saudi Arabia also realizes that Yemen's wish to keep its national independence acts as a counterbalance in preventing it from leaning too heavily toward the Soviet Union. In sum, Saudi Arabia attaches great importance to the political value of North Yemen to the Arabian Peninsula and the Gulf states and, further, considers instability in that country to be a major threat. Thus, an important policy goal of Saudi Arabia is to lessen tensions, increase dialogue and promote political cooperation with North Yemen.

Security Perceptions

Since its founding in 1932, the Kingdom of Saudi Arabia has evinced a remarkable record of internal stability, particularly for so volatile a region as the Middle East. To preserve this high degree of stability, Saudi Arabia has necessarily concerned itself with all real and potential subversive or insurgent activities occurring in the neighboring countries, of which North Yemen is one. The stakes are high, not only for the kingdom but also for the Free World, which is vitally interested in the uninterrupted flow of Saudi oil.[23]

Because of the spillover potential for violence and instability, Saudi Arabia believes that its internal security can be seriously affected by events elsewhere in the Middle East. As a result, the Saudis remain extremely attentive to the shifts in power and opinion in the countries which surround the kingdom. As a natural outgrowth of this line of reasoning, Saudi Arabia views events in North Yemen as having a major influence on Saudi internal security, whether positively or negatively.

As seen from the Saudi side, there are several ways in which North Yemen could exert a negative influence on the kingdom's internal stability. Further, it could exert this influence directly or indirectly, notwithstanding the consequences such actions would bring on itself.

One possible direct route to influence Saudi Arabia's stability negatively would be to use the work force present in Saudi Arabia to commit acts of sabotage or to organize and promote underground activities.[24] Saudi Arabia experienced this kind of situation during the Yemeni Civil War (1962–1970) when the Egyptians and the newly established republican regime in Sanaa pursued such a course.[25] Saudi vulnerability to these threats consist not so much in their chance of success but, rather, in the possible loss of its Yemeni work force resulting from the suspicion that would then befall it. Counterbalancing this potential for economic disruption, however, is the adverse economic effect pursuing such a course would have on the entire Yemen work force. Because the Yemenis lack alternative sources of employment at home and because of their dependence on transfer payments, a course of action with such a devastating impact on North Yemen's economy hardly seems attractive. As an example of the contribution Saudi employment makes to the Yemeni economy, 1978 figures show that Yemeni workers in Saudi Arabia sent home more than $1.5 billion.[26]

A second possible direct action by Yemen would be to smuggle infiltrators and weapons across the borders of North Yemen into Saudi Arabia. Well-trained infiltrators could inflict damage on vital and strategic military and civilian targets. However, this tactic, which was unsuccessfully tried in the 1960s, resulted in the Saudi execution of 17 Yemeni saboteurs.[27] Given this history, it seems unlikely to be tried again.

A third possible direct action would be to launch paramilitary attacks against cities and towns in the southern portion of Saudi Arabia. These attacks would entail an attempt to revive the old claim that part of Saudi Arabia's territory—particularly Jizan and Najran—actually belongs to North Yemen and should be returned to it. Ongoing border negotiations between Saudi Arabia and North Yemen have reduced the likelihood of this happening.[28]

Of course, the North Yemeni potential for causing trouble in Saudi Arabia is not limited to direct actions. Indirectly, problems might come from an anti-Saudi government. Such a government would de-emphasize Saudi-Yemeni relations and then cooperate with other anti-Saudi regimes in an effort to disrupt Saudi internal security.[29] Still another tactic might be to employ more Soviet and Eastern-bloc advisers. Such an action would lead to more communist influence in the Peninsula. Finally, North Yemen might intensify border hostilities. This would automatically disturb the security of the whole Arabian Peninsula.[30]

The types of actions described above undoubtedly would affect indirectly and negatively the security of Saudi Arabia. In so doing, they also would have a negative impact on the security of other Arab Gulf states as well. There are, of course, many constraints on such actions. One of the strongest is the good relations currently enjoyed by North Yemen and Saudi Arabia. Still another is the threat to Yemen's own self-interest. If Saudi Arabia were to expel its North Yemeni work force, the remittances, which are vitally needed back home, would cease. Saudi financial aid would also cease. These two consequences, taken together, could portend economic disaster for North Yemen.[31] Moreover, if Saudi Arabia found itself the target of such activities, almost certainly it would react with punitive measures of its own. Given its financial strength, Saudi Arabia would have the economic power to outbid the central government in Sanaa for the support of various sectors of the Yemeni population.

All in all, the constraints on such tactics rule out the present probability of their being used. As history has shown, however, conditions could change, and Saudi Arabia must therefore be prepared for all eventualities. Nevertheless, the greatest defense against potentially disruptive activities on the part of North Yemen is still a policy aimed at lessening tensions in the area and decreasing the need for Yemeni leaders to even consider such tactics.

Yemen is also in a position to play a positive role in enhancing the security of Saudi Arabia. Moreover, North Yemen is well aware that Saudi Arabia considers its own domestic stability to be intrinsically related to the foreign policy adopted by its neighbors. Given this understanding, North Yemen could contribute positively to enhancing that stability and security by conducting its own policies in a rational way. Such a positive role could be played first by developing closer relations with Saudi Arabia. This would involve its enhancing political, military and economic cooperation with the kingdom. To accomplish this, North Yemen would be required to place more trust in Saudi Arabia.[32] Second, North Yemen might lessen its dependence on communist bloc countries. Third, it could abandon its support for groups guided by radical and secular ideologies.[33] Fourth, it could establish good relations with the rest of the Arab Gulf countries.

Strategic Perceptions

The overriding concern of Saudi Arabian foreign policy remains the preservation of the Islamic way of life throughout the world. To promote this policy goal, Saudi Arabia has adopted both regional and international strategies which, though differing in focus, nevertheless complement one another.

Saudi Arabia's regional strategy rests on the premise that the Arab world, and particularly the Arabian Gulf and Peninsula states, must assume first priority in its foreign policy. The primary Saudi policy goal is the achievement and maintenance of peace and stability in the region through the exercise of moderation and rationality. Saudi Arabia detects three main threats to regional peace and stability: Soviet-Marxist expansionism; Zionist expansionism; and the unrest caused by the thwarted aspirations of the Arab people—economically, because they lack domestic opportunities, and politically, because of their inability to end the Zionist threat.[34]

During the 1960s and early 1970s, Saudi Arabia had limited financial resources, limited global political influence and limited military power. These limitations prevented it from adopting an active regional policy to defend against threats. The quadrupling of oil prices in 1973–1974, however, and the emergence of Saudi Arabia as the Free World's key oil-producing country changed all this. Saudi Arabia's newly gained wealth and prominence soon enabled it to become the leader of the moderate Arab states.[35] As such, by the mid-1970s the kingdom had developed a two-pronged national strategy. The first prong involved the use of large-scale economic aid to reduce Soviet influence wherever possible. The second called for the rapid development of a reliable domestic defense of its own.

To achieve its first aim—the reduction of Soviet influence through economic aid—since the mid-1970s the kingdom has allocated up to eight percent of its gross national product (GNP) for foreign aid. In 1978, Saudi Arabia allocated $5.5 billion in foreign aid, equal to 8.45 percent of its GNP.[36] To achieve the second aim, the kingdom has accelerated and expanded military development programs begun in the 1960s. As an example of its determination to develop an advanced defense system, the kingdom has purchased F15 fighters and AWACS, airborne early-warning aircraft. Its allocation for the defense budget in 1980 alone was approximately $18 billion.[37]

In an effort to enhance regional, political, economic and military cooperation, Saudi Arabia has strongly supported the formation of the Gulf Cooperation Council (GCC), which was created on May 25, 1981. If formation of the GCC indicates anything, it is agreement among its members (i.e., Saudi Arabia, Kuwait, Bahrain, Qatar, the United Arab Emirates and Oman) that a broadly based cooperative effort is necessary to cope with potential external threats against each state. Despite the initial emphasis on economic, educational and social cooperation, mutual military security was the principal reason for establishing the Council.[38]

With regard to the Palestinian question, Saudi Arabia is anxious to see that a just and peaceful solution to that question is found. In great part, the importance attached to the Palestinian issue stems from its belief that the Arab-Israeli conflict presents the major obstacle to peace and stability in the region. Saudi Arabia firmly believes that resolving the Palestinian question is the key to establishing stability and security throughout the Arab world.[39] To promote its goal of attaining a just solution to the Palestinian question, Saudi Arabia attempted to break the political impasse which had developed on the issue. It did this by putting forth the "Fahd Peace Plan" in August 1981 as an alternative to the Camp David Accords. Those accords, which brought peace only to Egypt and Israel and which did not address the Palestinian situation, were rejected shortly thereafter by the Arab world.[40]

Another important feature of the Saudi regional strategic policy is its activist efforts to contain regional conflicts throughout the Arab world and most particularly in the Arabian Peninsula. Saudi Arabia has been a principal mediator in most of the conflicts that have developed among Arab states. These have included efforts to end or at least reduce tensions in the Iraqi-Kuwaiti dispute, the North-South Yemeni border conflicts, the Algerian-Moroccan dispute over the Western Sahara, the South-Yemeni-supported insurgency in Oman's Dhofar province, and the Iraqi-Syrian dispute.[41]

Although the Soviet threat is worldwide, the Saudi response to it, as befits the kingdom's limited resources, has been regional in scope. It focuses on diverting Soviet or Soviet-supported threats on the Red Sea, the Indian Ocean and the Arabian Gulf. As a means of keeping Soviet influence out of the region, the kingdom has adopted a neutral policy of discouraging any kind of fixed military presence in the region by either of the superpowers. This Saudi position has been made clear by His Majesty King Fahd and the Saudi foreign minister, Prince Saud al-Faisal.[42]

Containing the spread of Soviet-supported, radical political ideologies and preventing Soviet political penetration and influence in the region have been as important a part of Saudi regional policy as its opposition to military and security threats.[43] In fact, radicalism and Soviet penetration, particularly in the Arabian Peninsula, are regarded by Saudi Arabia as major threats to the entire Arab world.

North Yemen's important position in Saudi regional strategy has been determined both by its being a neighbor of the kingdom and by its being accorded a high priority in Soviet expansionist plans.[44] Given its paramountcy, North Yemen's cooperation with Saudi regional strategy would significantly enhance its chances for success. For example, if North Yemen succeeded in stabilizing its internal security situation and ended its border conflicts with South Yemen, the prospects for peace and stability in the whole Arabian Peninsula would thereby be enhanced, and the threat of Soviet hegemony correspondingly would be reduced. Moreover, if North Yemen were to adopt a neutral policy with regard to superpower presence in the Indian Ocean and the Red Sea area, the Saudi regional strategy might achieve yet another measure of success. Likewise, if North Yemen supported Saudi political initiatives on the Palestinian question and other regional issues, the chances for regional peace and stability would be greatly increased.

Since North Yemen remains vulnerable to external political, economic, and ideological pressures because of its economic and social needs, Saudi Arabia likely would welcome increased Yemeni dependence on Saudi financial and developmental aid. Such increased Saudi dependence would replace aid coming from ideologically oriented countries, such as the Soviet Union and Red China. Such a development would be a major victory for Saudi regional strategy and would enhance the Saudi-led Arab moderation throughout the Arab world. In sum, North Yemen fits deeply and strongly into Saudi regional strategy and is highly regarded by Saudi decisionmakers.

North Yemen fits into Saudi Arabia's Islamic strategy because it embodies an Islamic state by virtue of its culture, traditions and population. As such, Saudi Arabia considers North Yemen to be an important component of its strategy and a country which should act as a good Islamic role model for the rest of the world. In this respect, Saudi Arabia has not been disappointed in North Yemen. Islamic law and Islamic judiciary systems are preserved by North Yemen, as is Islamic education. These undertakings by North Yemen are made easier because, as a Muslim country, North Yemen has received Saudi financial aid allocated to Islamic nations.[45] Thus, by actively promoting Islamic values, North Yemen has made an important contribution to advancing Saudi policies in the Islamic world. Saudi Arabia, in turn, appreciates the value of North Yemeni support and hopes for its continued implementation.

Saudi Arabia believes that, despite differences in economic and political interests, amiable relations with the Western industrialized countries offer it and its neighbors—including North Yemen—the best hope for realizing economic development and preserving their freedom from communism. One important way in which Saudi Arabia helps to foster good relations with the West is by using its position as the Free World's key oil producer, and hence possessor of huge foreign-exchange holdings, to maintain a stable world oil market and by pursuing international fiscal and monetary policies which will help rather than hinder the flow of goods and services.

Because of the political differences between the Arab world and the industrialized world, particularly over the Arab-Israeli problem, the kingdom has had a difficult time convincing North Yemen openly to adopt similar pro-Western policies. Despite this difficulty, however, North Yemen has been in fact a pro-Western country to some extent.

Trade relations with the British and technical and economic relations with the United States have characterized North Yemen's relations with the Western world during the 1970s. Recent statistics published by the Y.A.R. Central Bank showed that in addition to Saudi Arabia, all North Yemen's main trading partners were Western-aligned countries.[46] This trade profile unquestionably correlates with Saudi policy toward the industrialized world. Nevertheless, North Yemen still maintains relations with the Soviet Union in hopes of playing East off against West—a strategy which can prove dangerous. If North Yemen loses some of its freedom to the Soviets, the entire Arabian Peninsula will suffer as a result.

The kingdom shares with the Western industrialized countries several other political goals. One goal is to preserve peace and stability in the Arabian Peninsula as a whole. A second goal is to prevent communism from infiltrating the Arab world, particularly the Arabian Peninsula. A third goal is to maintain peace and security in the Third World.[47] Moreover, Saudi Arabia views a strong United States and Free World as the underpinning of the West's will and ability to contain communism and other radical forces. Furthermore, Saudi Arabia considers it the West's responsibility to show resolve in meeting destabilizing threats to the region, whether they come from communism or Zionism.

North Yemen shares little of this policy with Saudi Arabia. Although North Yemen is considered a pro-Western country, it apparently does not recognize communism as a threat to Yemen or the Arabian Peninsula in the same way that Saudi Arabia does. Consequently, it does not share the Saudi perspective of a strong United States and Free World being the underpinning of the West's will and ability to contain communism and other radical forces.

Despite its failure to recognize communism as a real threat and to take steps accordingly, there are those analysts who argue that as long as the tribes are powerful in North Yemen, communism will make no inroads into the country and the Soviets will not realize their goal of dominating the country. Be that as it may, Saudi Arabia hopes that one day rationality and wisdom, not ideology, will dominate the policymaking apparatus of North Yemen and thereby end what Saudi Arabia sees as a dangerous flirtation with the Soviet Union. Though this hope may be criticized as wishful thinking on the part of Saudi Arabia, Saudi policymakers counter that the Islamic nature of Arab political history has proven that this is the nature of "Arabpolitik."

Since the unrest caused by the ongoing Palestinian question poses not only a regional threat but an international threat to the world's oil and economic system, the Saudi objective in reaching a peaceful solution to this question is part of its international strategy as well. Saudi Arabia therefore strives to gain the support of the industrialized countries, particularly the United States, to use their power and influence to find a just and peaceful solution to the Palestinian question. Indeed, the kingdom believes that the only hope for continuing stability in the Middle East lies in resolving the Palestinian question.[48] North Yemen seems to be in agreement with this part of Saudi Arabia's position over the need for Western support to resolve the Palestinian problem.

In sum, Saudi Arabia believes that if North Yemen were to develop closer relations with the industrialized world, Saudi policy would be greatly enhanced. At the same time, the kingdom believes that North

Yemen cannot continue to ignore Western power or the fact that communism presents the greatest threat to regional stability.

Saudi policy toward the Third World aims at assisting Third World countries to develop their own resources in order to insure their political and economic stability and lessen the threat of communist expansion. The Saudis have therefore allocated an enormous amount of aid to those countries. For example, Saudi Arabia pledged nearly $1 billion to the African countries immediately after the Afro-Arab summit in Cairo in March 1977.

North Yemen not only is a regional Arab state with an Islamic society but, as a developing country, it falls within the sphere of Saudi Arabia's Third World policies as well. North Yemen has been the recipient of considerable Saudi financial support without which it is difficult to see how the government could survive. Saudi Arabia has annually provided North Yemen with more than a third of official Saudi foreign aid expenditures. In addition, Saudi Arabia has financed many of its development projects.[49]

In addition, North Yemeni relations with other Third World countries parallel Saudi relations in many respects. For example, North Yemen maintains good relations with moderate African as well as Asian countries. This coincides with Saudi policies, and North Yemen's stand is viewed by Saudi Arabia as a positive one. Regional and international peace and stability work to the advantage of all Third World countries. Therefore, Saudi Arabia will continue to seek the cooperation of North Yemen regardless of the particular problems or successes characterizing their relations at any particular time.

Lessons of the Civil War

A country such as Egypt, with its strategic location in the Middle East, its long and glorious history and its extensive manpower base, was unfortunately led by Nasser and his unrealistic policies into a foreign civil-war situation that not only contributed to the deterioration of its army but also depleted the country's resources. Nasser was defeated in Yemen despite an enormous military and financial investment. He apparently miscalculated the costs of a Yemen adventure, regarding intervention there as an easy task. He sent troops to fight a war in an area which was completely foreign to them. The result was the loss of approximately 26,000 Egyptian lives. In the process, he led his country into economic difficulties of such magnitude as to cause harm to Egypt's entire economy. Egypt still suffers from the effects of that adventure today. Moreover, by shifting his attention to the Yemen front, the Israeli-Egyptian front was left "unguarded," a liability which the Israelis were able to take advantage of in June 1967 by destroying nearly all of Egypt's air force and inflicting a bitter defeat on the Egyptian army. In short, Nasser deceived himself and his nation by intervening in Yemen. Yemen actually became Nasser's "Vietnam," as he himself acknowledged in 1964.

Throughout his rule over Egypt (1954–1970), Nasser spoke of "revolution" in the Arab world. What constitutes a "revolution?" Michael C. Hudson provides insight for this query as he writes:

> If the term revolution is understood in its most profound sense, as an upheaval that not only overturns a political regime but also changes social, cultural values and distribution of wealth, then one could argue whether the Arabs have experienced any revolution at all.[50]

In the case of North Yemen, the 1962 revolution created a new political culture without a logical or even a contrived focus. In the meantime, neither socio-economic development nor political stability was achieved promptly, due to the failure of successive governments to overcome factionalism and personal ambitions, as well as because of their lack of legitimacy.[51]

In this respect, Yemeni scholar Mohammad A. Zabarah has cogently observed that:

> Revolutions have as their primary objectives the transformation of society. They aim to fundamentally change the social living habits and values of the larger part of society. They are distinct from coup d'état or palace revolutions in that a coup d'état merely changes the people in power or a few laws.[52]

On balance, Zabarah sees the Yemeni Revolution of 1962 as a social revolution which achieved considerable and remarkable changes in Yemeni society. His argument largely concerns the open-door policy of the government, the progress in the economic field and in education, and the emergence of women as a "work force" in development plans. But it remains debatable whether or not this is sufficient to characterize Yemen as a revolutionary country. At the same time, it is difficult to refute the argument that Yemeni society is still, and will likely remain for some years to come, basically "tribal." The tribes in Yemen constitute some 95 percent of the total population. They embody the most powerful political and military force in Yemen, and their domestic influence undoubtedly will remain formidable for decades to come.[53]

In short, the Yemeni takeover of 1962 cannot be characterized as revolution in the strict sense of the term. Nevertheless, for Pan-Arabists such as Nasser, these political events were classified as revolutions, largely to influence the Arab masses. The term "revolution," therefore, was abused and employed as propaganda by Nasser and his supporters in the Arab world.

In addition to Arab factors, the Yemen crisis involved both the United States and the Soviet Union. The former tried its utmost to avoid military confrontation between Saudi Arabia and Egypt, whereas the latter tried to take advantage of the situation and establish a "foothold" in Yemen. As a bottom line, however, both superpowers exercised considerable restraint, although neither was willing to allow the other to gain any significant military or moral victory.

The involvement of regional and international organizations, particularly the Arab League and the United Nations, produced several general conclusions for conflict resolution. First, cooperation of the parties concerned is a vital element for the success of any mediation effort. Second, as with most problems that regional and international organizations confront, the Yemeni dilemma had become virtually unsolvable by the time it had reached the Arab League and the United Nations. Third, mediation efforts by third parties can temporarily lessen tensions, but any final solution must rest with the parties concerned. Last, but not least, troubled nations hold the key to their problems' solution, and they alone can usually determine their future course in a conflict.

Nonetheless, and in all fairness to the Arab League and the United Nations, these organizations are "forums," rather than "actors." Their achievements depend on the degree to which sovereign states, in which the real political power resides, are willing to live up to the obligations of their charters. However, the slow procedures and bureaucratic delays exercised by both the Arab League's and the United Nation's respective offices contributed to their slowness of action in the Yemen crisis. Consequently, this complicated the situation and made it more difficult to arrive at an early solution of the Yemeni crisis. On the other hand, states must have more confidence in the organizations they have created and in their respective offices. This step naturally should facilitate the job of secretaries-general and encourage them to take actions which will serve the peaceful and moral tasks of these organizations.

There is no doubt that the pre-1962 situation in Yemen—socially, economically, and politically—was unique and unfavorable. Yemen was one of the most backward countries, not only within the Arabian Peninsula, but also among all Middle Eastern countries. Yemenis in general and the military establishment in particular were always eager to express their views to the ruling Hamid al-Din family, as well as anxious to put an end to Yemen's isolation.[54] Moreover, it was obvious that deep misunderstandings existed between the Hamid al-Din family and the Yemeni people. Inevitably, clashes arose and attempts against the regime were made and repressed. The royal family believed that it could rule the Yemeni people with "iron and fire," whereas the Yemeni people began to feel they could not achieve their freedom without removing the royal family. Consequently, a huge gap of mutual misunderstanding and mistrust was created over a number of decades that eventually made it impossible for both parties to overcome the "high wall" of obstacles.

The 1948 assassination of Imam Yahya, followed by Abdallah al-Wazir's attempt to seize power, failed again in bringing the two sides together. When Imam Ahmad succeeded his father (Imam Yahya) following the 1948 attempt, his policies too were unacceptable to many of his subjects. Resorting to traditional means of governing, Imam Ahmad ruled his people much as his father had. By doing so, he ignored the new elements that had been introduced to the Yemeni society in the 1940s and 1950s, namely, the emergence of university graduates, military groups and emigrant workers, who wanted to see a change in Yemen's internal and external outlook. The Imam's attitude almost cost him his throne and life in 1955 and 1961.

After he regained his throne in the 1955 attempted coup, he made no effort to change internal policies in such a way that they would have made him more acceptable to the Yemeni people. Thus, the tensions between the ruler and the ruled continued until the successful coup d'état of 1962.

Finally, the descriptions of the Yemen war as the "Unknown War" and as the "Undeclared War"[55] carry some degree of truth. Despite the fact that the Yemen crisis could have engulfed all the Arabian Peninsula in open conflict—which would have adversely affected the interests of the Western world in the region—not many people have heard of it, and even less have paid close attention to it. In summation, given the background of the war and the serious involvement of outside parties, probably the most apt description for the Yemeni conflict might be the "Unwinnable Ideological War."

Conclusion

In the final analysis, one may conclude that the five key points mentioned in the early stages of this work have been proven valid. Without Egypt's anti-Imamate campaign, its initial support to the plotters, and its participation indirectly in the palace bombardment by putting some of the tanks and military vehicles into operation, the coup d'état could have been unsuccessful and could have been easily contained by the Imam and his personal guards who fought with him for 24 hours against the rebels. Moreover, if Egypt had not interfered militarily in the days following the coup, using professional soldiers and sophisticated weapons, the coup d'état certainly would have failed, and the rebels would have been unable to control the major cities of Yemen.

With regard to the second key point, it has been made clear by the Saudi officials quoted above that the Saudi involvement was prompted by hostile Egyptian and Yemeni republican attitudes, as well as the Imam's personal request for assistance. Therefore, Saudi Arabia's role was purely defensive, and the kingdom never engaged in military operations against the Egyptians or the republicans inside Yemen. Saudi Arabia acted only to prevent Egyptian/Yemeni threats to its southern borders.

The above observations underscore the third key point, that North Yemen is an important asset to Saudi Arabia. One must acknowledge the fact that North Yemen is militarily important to the Kingdom of Saudi Arabia. First, a strong North Yemeni military force favorable to Saudi Arabia could form a deterrent force against any potential or real threat to Saudi Arabia by the Marxist-Leninist government of South Yemen. Second, hostile navy vessels aiming at Saudi seaports and coming through Bab al-Mandab could be stopped before reaching their targets, from North Yemen's seaports, such as al-Hudaydah, and other islands and areas belonging to North Yemen and overlooking the Red Sea, such as Kamaran Island and Dubab area. Third, North Yemen, in the case of a military conflict between Saudi Arabia and the Marxist regime in South Yemen, could serve as a supply base for the kingdom and would enable it to encircle South Yemen from both the north and the northwest borders. For these reasons, Saudi Arabia must pay close attention to North Yemen's internal security, foreign policy, and ideological orientation, even though it is well known that the kingdom does not intervene in the domestic policies and affairs of other nations.

The fourth key point proven to be valid was that the conduct of both the United States and the Soviet Union in the Yemeni crisis was determined by their regional interest. The Yemen case of 1962, in fact, was a test for the superpowers' rivalry in the Middle East, in general, and the Arabian Peninsula, in particular.

The fifth and final key point was proved to be true since none of the mediation efforts, whether by regional and international organizations or by individual countries, was successful in ending the conflict in Yemen. Only Yemenis themselves were able to find a solution to their problem. Mediation efforts exerted and conducted by outsiders only helped to lessen the tensions but did not bring an end to the conflict.

In its approach to the problems posed by the coup in Yemen and Egyptian intervention, the government of Saudi Arabia pursued a multifaceted policy. While calling for an end to the civil war and formally declaring its neutrality, the Kingdom of Saudi Arabia tilted heavily toward the royalist forces under the leadership of the ex-Imam. This tilting, however, was seen by the kingdom as a strategic necessity to divert the Yemeni-Egyptian threat on its southern border. Nevertheless, this action was seen by pro-republican Yemenis as interference in Yemen's domestic affairs.

Accordingly, republican Yemen did not take advantage of Saudi neutrality in the early months of the revolution. Instead, it aligned itself with Egypt and began attacking the Saudi monarchy. In addition, republican Yemen tilted towards the Soviet Union and the Eastern-bloc countries. Consequently, these actions prompted Saudi—as well as Western (particularly the United States and Great Britain)—suspicion of the republican regime's intentions. From the Saudi point of view, such policy on the part of republican Yemen constituted a potential threat to the kingdom itself and the whole Arabian Peninsula. The same feeling was later shared by a number of prominent Yemeni republicans who at the end of 1964 withdrew from the republican ranks, formed their own political force and joined the Saudi efforts to neutralize Yemen and give the chance to Yemenis to choose their own form of government.

Throughout the interviews that were conducted by the author, incumbent as well as ex-Saudi, Yemeni and Egyptian officials emphasized the fact that the Yemeni dilemma could have been prevented if Egyptian military intervention had not materialized and Saudi assistance to the royalists had not taken place. The Egyptian action, according to Mahmoud Riad, was justified as a result of Egypt's leading revolutionary role in the Arab world. The Saudi action, according to Saudi officials, was justified as a consequence of North Yemen's importance to the security and stability of the kingdom itself and the Arabian Peninsula as a whole. Nevertheless, the ex-Imam affirmed that if the rebels had not been backed by Egyptian troops, he and his followers could have suppressed the coup, and he would have regained his throne.

On balance, the Yemeni dilemma from 1962 to 1970 was a lesson for all Arab states striving for power and influence in the Arab world. It manifested how a small country, by embroiling big powers in a fruitless conflict, can endanger the security of regional and international peace and order.

Notes

[1] Margarita Dobert, "Development of Aid Programs to Yemen," *American-Arab Affairs*, no. 8 (Spring 1984), p. 115.

² Anthony H. Cordesman, *The Gulf and the Search for Strategic Stability: Saudi Arabia, the Military Balance in the Gulf, and Trends in the Arab-Israeli Military Balance* (Boulder, CO: Westview Press, 1984), p. 467.

³ Fouad al-Farsy, *Saudi Arabia: A Case Study in Development* (London: Stacey International, 1980), pp. 89–91.

⁴ David E. Long, "Kingdom of Saudi Arabia," in David E. Long and Bernard Reich, eds., *The Government and Politics of the Middle East and North Africa* (Boulder, CO: Westview Press, 1980), pp. 102–103.

⁵ J. E. Peterson, *Yemen: The Search for a Modern State* (Baltimore: The Johns Hopkins University Press, 1982), p. 108.

⁶ William B. Quandt, *Saudi Arabia in the 1980s: Foreign Policy, Security, and Oil* (Washington, DC: The Brookings Institution, 1981), p. 10.

⁷ John Shaw and David E. Long, *Saudi Arabian Modernization: The Impact of Change on Stability* (New York: Praeger, for the Center for Strategic and International Studies, Georgetown University, Washington Paper No. 89, 1982), pp. 35–40.

⁸ David McClintock, "The Yemen Arab Republic," in Long and Reich, p. 176.

⁹ Peterson, pp. 172–173.

¹⁰ Ibid., pp. 184–188, 172.

¹¹ *Middle East Business Survey* (Washington, DC: National Association of Arab Americans, 1982), p. 65.

¹² South Yemen is the only country in the Arabian Peninsula which did not benefit greatly from that wealth, although some South Yemenis have worked in the Gulf states. This is a result of its dependence on communist bloc countries and its centrally planned economic system.

¹³ Robin Bidwell, *The Two Yemens* (Boulder, CO: Westview Press, 1983), pp. 327–328.

¹⁴ Robert W. Stookey, *Yemen: The Politics of the Yemen Arab Republic* (Boulder, CO: Westview Press, 1978), p. 275–276.

¹⁵ Yemenis apparently feel that by playing one side off against another they can get more financial aid from Saudi Arabia and more military aid from the United States. They know of the Saudi-American concern about the presence of the Soviet Union in South Yemen and are taking advantage of this. They try to manipulate the two countries to achieve their own goals.

¹⁶ There are approximately 70,000 Palestinians in Saudi Arabia and about 4,000 in North Yemen according to a prominent Saudi official.

¹⁷ "The Dilemmas of the U.S. Policy Towards the Gulf," *Institute for Defense Studies and Analyses Journal* (IDSA Journal), vol. 12, no. 1 (July-September 1979), p. 113.

¹⁸ There are approximately 500,000 North Yemenis working in Saudi Arabia and about 150,000 in various other Arab Gulf states.

¹⁹ This feeling became obvious after the 1962 coup d'état in North Yemen, which was followed by the Egyptian intervention and the statements of Yemen's new leaders that they intended to destabilize the entire Arabian Peninsula and to support anti-monarchial groups in Saudi Arabia and the Gulf as well.

[20] Much of North Yemen fell under Turkish control between 1872 and 1918. The Turks and the British clashed over control of Yemen, which resulted in the creation of the Aden Protectorate by the British, dividing Yemen into North and South. North Yemen then remained under the Turks until 1918, when the Hamid al-Din family came to power and ruled Yemen until the 1962 revolution. During the so-called revolutionary era, since 1962, North Yemen has had five presidents, nearly all of them removed by force, and thirteen premiers. Compared to the situation under the Imamate system, the republican leadership has been much less stable, though perhaps no less tranquil. For more details, see Bidwell, pp. 44–49, 263–282, 321–324.

[21] Oil has, however, recently been discovered in North Yemen in limited commercial quantities.

[22] Besides Saudi opposition, tribal power and the Islamic nature of North Yemen provide obstacles to Soviet penetration of North Yemen.

[23] Cordesman, p. 3.

[24] Quandt, p. 27.

[25] David Holden and Richard Johns, *The House of Saud* (New York: Holt, Rinehart and Winston, 1981), p. 250.

[26] Bidwell, p. 295.

[27] Robert Lacey, *The Kingdom: Arabia & the House of Sa'ud* (New York: Avon Books, 1981), p. 381.

[28] Currently, Saudi and Yemeni officials are negotiating the issue of Jizan and Najran in accordance with the articles of the 1934 Taif Treaty.

[29] North Yemen could cooperate either with South Yemen or with the Soviet Union or even with Libya to disturb the internal security of the kingdom.

[30] When the two Yemens engaged in a border war in February and March 1979, Saudi Arabia and other Arab Gulf states were so concerned that they were willing to intervene militarily if peaceful efforts failed. See Cordesman, pp. 449–455.

[31] In July 1970, Saudi Arabia recognized the republican regime in Sanaa and a Saudi-Yemeni "Coordinated Committee" was formed to channel Saudi economic and military funds to Sanaa. This Committee was chaired by Prince Sultan ibn Abd al-Aziz, the Saudi defense minister. See Cordesman, p. 467.

[32] When asked about Saudi-Yemeni relations in an interview given on December 29, 1984, to the correspondent of the Kuwait newspaper, *Al-Ray al-Am*, President Ali Abdallah Salih of North Yemen responded, "Our relationship with the Kingdom of Saudi Arabia is unique and friendly. It is developing continuously in the different fields of coordination to serve the bright mutual goals of the two nations; . . . it receives the appreciation of the Yemeni people for the great support and generosity that is extended to our country in the field of development."

[33] Despite the fact that North Yemen is a Muslim country, there are Yemenis who belong to different ideological camps, such as the Baath Party in Iraq, the Nasserites in Egypt and the communists in South Yemen.

[34] David E. Long, *The United States and Saudi Arabia: Ambivalent Allies* (Boulder, CO: Westview Press, 1985), pp. 3–8.

35 Ibid., p. 3.

36 Organization for Economic Cooperation and Development Assistance Committee, *Development Cooperation Efforts, 1982 Review*, cited in J. E. Peterson, ed., *The Politics of Middle Eastern Oil* (Washington, DC: Middle East Institute, 1983), p. 462.

37 Enver M. Koury, "The Impact of the Geopolitical Situation of Iraq upon the Gulf Cooperation Council," *Middle East Insight*, vol. 2, no. 5 (1983), p. 31.

38 Wahib Muhammad Ghurab, "The Second Gulf Summit" (in Arabic), *Al-Majallah*, no. 93 (November 21–22, 1982), p. 27.

39 John C. Campbell, "The Middle East: A House of Containment Built on Shifting Sands," in *Foreign Affairs*; Special Issue on "America and the World, 1981," p. 605.

40 George Rentz, "The Fahd Peace Plan," *Middle East Insight*, vol. 2, no. 2 (1983), p. 21.

41 Nabeel A. Khoury, "The Pragmatic Trend in Inter-Arab Politics," *The Middle East Journal*, vol. 36, no. 3 (Summer 1982), p. 379.

42 *Al-Majallah*, No. 65 (May 9–15, 1983), pp. 3–5.

43 Robert R. Sullivan, "Saudi Arabia in International Politics," *Review of Politics*, vol. 28 (1979), pp. 436–460.

44 David Lynn Price, "Moscow and the Persian Gulf," *Problems of Communism*, vol. 28 (March-April 1979), p. 1.

45 North Yemen alone received 810 million Saudi riyals in 1981 for development projects according to a senior Saudi official.

46 Bidwell, pp. 282–284.

47 Jean Pierre Cot, "Winning East-West in North-South," *Foreign Policy*, no. 46 (Spring 1982), p. 12.

48 William B. Quandt, "Saudi Arabia Security and Foreign Policy in the 1980s," *Middle East Insight*, vol. 2, no. 2 (1983), p. 29.

49 Bidwell, p. 294.

50 Michael C. Hudson, *Arab Politics: The Search for Legitimacy* (New Haven: Yale University Press, 1977), pp. 232–233.

51 J. E. Peterson, p. 172.

52 Mohammed A. Zabarah, "The Yemeni Revolution of 1962 Seen as a Social Revolution," paper presented at the international Symposium on Contemporary Yemen, Exeter, England, July 15–18, 1983, pp. 1–2.

53 A prominent Saudi politician who is involved in the Saudi policymaking *vis-à-vis* North Yemen.

54 It is very interesting to note here, based on the author's experience, that the Yemeni tribes are the most eager party in practicing democracy through an electoral college, consultative assembly and people's council.

55 Dana Adams Schmidt, *Yemen: The Unknown War* (New York: Holt, Rinehart and Winston, 1968); and "The Undeclared War," *The New Republic*, no. 149 (August 3, 1963), pp. 8–9.

Appendix 1

A HISTORICAL DOCUMENT WRITTEN BY H.M. IMAM MUHAMMAD AL-BADR CONCERNING THE COUP D'ETAT AGAINST HIM

London; March 10, 1985

In the Name of God, the Most Gracious, Most Merciful

This is a historical document that explains my viewpoint with regard to the military coup d'état that took place against my government and family in September 1962.

Abd al-Nasser's biggest historical mistake was his military intervention in Yemen's affairs. The Egyptian media—whether press, or broadcasting or television—concentrated on supporting the military-socialist system of Egypt against the other existing systems in the Arab world, including the Imamate in Yemen.

Regarding Saudi support for Yemen, there was no intervention by the Kingdom of Saudi Arabia in Yemen's affairs. What really happened is that, when the bloody events took place in Sanaa, the Yemeni people revolted, and the Egyptian intervention then took place against the Yemeni people. Then came Amer and his sort who warned and threatened. Therefore, the Kingdom of Saudi Arabia was forced to defend itself, and according to its Islamic duties, the kingdom was helping Yemen. As King Faisal, God rest his soul, said in his speech in Taif, "We help the nation of Yemen by satisfying the filling of the two stomachs, the human stomach so that it does not die from hunger and the gun's stomach with which it defends itself and its country."

As for my impressions about the political situation during the period from 1956 to 1965 in the Arab world, it was a period of travail and waiting. President Abd al-Nasser was riding the Soviet wheel and wanted to imprint the Arab world with his own seal. Time has unmasked him in Egypt itself and proven him wrong in choosing that path, as Egypt's writers and scholars have written.

In my soul, I knew King Faisal, God rest his soul, from near and far. I knew of his loyalty to God, the nation, Islam and Arabism.

As for my feelings toward Abd al-Nasser, I liked and respected him, and there was friendship between us. But, unfortunately, he destroyed that friendship and betrayed it. He blindly followed the propagandists and demagogues.

(Signed)
(Imam) Muhammad al-Badr

Appendix 2

AN INTERVIEW WITH H.M. IMAM MUHAMMAD AL-BADR (THE FORMER RULER OF NORTH YEMEN)

METHODOLOGY: Questions were prepared in advance by the author and written down in Arabic. At the interview, these written questions were submitted to the interviewee, who responded orally in Arabic. The interviewee was permitted to answer uninterrupted, for as long as he deemed it necessary to respond to the question. The author took notes on his answers; no taping of answers was done. After the interview, the author translated his notes on the interviewee's responses into English. The interviewee was not asked to approve the translation.

Bromley South, London

Wednesday, December 21, 1983

Q.1. It was said that President Nasser of Egypt began brainwashing the military Yemeni personnel since the 1958 unity agreement between Egypt, Syria and North Yemen. What is your Majesty's comment on this?

A.1. It is true that Abd al-Nasser was working to achieve this goal. However, he started moving in this direction in 1960, particularly after my rejection of his offer to cooperate with him in overthrowing the Saudi regime as a step toward controlling the Arabian Peninsula. Nevertheless, the brainwashing of the Yemenis, the military as well as the youth, had been carried out by the Islamic Center (in Cairo) then headed by Anwar al-Sadat. Secret contacts with Yemenis were conducted by this Center inside and outside Yemen under many Islamic slogans. In the meantime, Abd al-Rahman al-Baidani, who is originally an

117

Egyptian and married to the sister of al-Sadat's wife, had played a vital role in this direction too, i.e., brainwashing the Yemenis.

Q.2. It has been mentioned in a number of books written about North Yemen that President Nasser is the one who planned for the coup d'état from Cairo and Sanaa. What is the truth about this?

A.2. This is true. There was an Egyptian diplomat called Muhammad Abd al-Waled working at the Egyptian Embassy in Sanaa. He had more authority than the Ambassador Ahmad Abu Zayd. In fact, this Abd al-Waled was the representative of Egyptian intelligence in Yemen, and used to encourage the Yemenis to carry out demonstrations and conducted acts of violence against the rule of my father, the late Imam Ahmad. My father used to tell Abu Zayd frankly, "I don't like you. I always suspect you, and I suspect your behavior and motives."

Q.3. It was said that Abdallah al-Sallal was in touch with the Egyptian military attaché in Sanaa, and that a number of Egyptian military personnel had helped in fixing some of the armored vehicles which bombarded and attacked the royal palace on the evening of the coup d'état. What is the truth of this story?

A.3. This is not true. As you know, the Yemeni forces were trained by the Egyptian experts and advisers. When these advisers left Yemen, all military equipment was in good operational shape. However, in the early morning following the coup d'état, and during the time of my counterattack against the rebels, which lasted about 24 hours, my supporters and I saw some helicopters landing near the palace and in the vicinity of Sanaa airport. To me, this meant either that the helicopters were on board ships anchored near the Yemeni coast or they were assembled inside the Egyptian Embassy in Sanaa.

Q.4. Then, how did the coup d'état take place and who was its Yemeni leader?

A.4. On the evening of the coup d'état, I was presiding over the new Council of Ministers located inside the Royal Palace compound. The meeting ended late at night because many affairs and subjects had to be discussed. While I was walking towards the residential palace, an officer called Hussein al-Sukary, who was a deputy to al-Sallal in providing security for the royal palace, tried to assassinate me from behind but the rifle's trigger jammed. While my personal guards were trying to arrest him, he shot himself in the chin. He is still alive today, but with a disfigured face. Al-Sallal himself was neither in the meeting hall nor in the palace at the time. I continued my walk toward the residential palace. After resting for awhile, the electricity was cut off and I felt that something wrong was going on. This was followed by gunfire on the palace. I then began with my personal guards and the guards of the palace to fire back. In fact, the ringleader of the coup and its principal Yemeni planner was an officer called Abd al-Ghani who was killed during the early hours of the coup. It is possible that he was the one who had constant contact with the Egyptian Embassy in Sanaa.

Q.5. What was the impact of Nasser's intervention in Yemen and his support to the republicans?

A.5. If Nasser had not interfered in Yemen and had not supported the rebels, I would have been able, along with my supporters, to control the situation easily. Even after my departure from Sanaa while I headed toward the northern part of the country, specifically toward Amran and al-Khobah, all tribes of that region rallied to me and stood by my side. They numbered 15,000 armed and unarmed men. But even those armed men were armed with personal and old weapons and needed modern weapons to counter the Egyptian troops in Yemen. This reason, in fact, led me to proceed towards the Saudi borders and seek help from the late King Saud.

Q.6. The Egyptian news media at that time, 1962, claimed that it was the Saudi intervention in Yemen which made Nasser make the decision to interfere in Yemen to protect its revolution, and that the same Saudi intervention was responsible for the outbreak of the Yemeni Civil War. What is Your Majesty's view?

A.6. This is not true. As I mentioned earlier, the Egyptian helicopters landed in Sanaa on the morning following the coup d'état, and my contact with the late King Saud did not materialize until I reached al-Mahabshah on the Yemeni-Saudi borders along with my supporters. From there, I contacted the late King, who sent me two of the Sudairi brothers, Ahmed and Turki. They asked me what I wanted from the kingdom. I answered that I wanted the kingdom to help and assist me in arming my followers to fight back the rebels and their Egyptian supporters, to regain my throne. After several days, I received King Saud's approval of my request, and the process of arming my supporters started. We first armed seven thousand men (7,000), and the rest were armed in groupings. In fact, most of the tribes were willing to leave their homes and lands to join me, and the Egyptians, themselves, wanted them to do so to be able to control the whole country. But, I asked them to stay inside Yemen and began arming them with Saudi Arabia's help in accordance with my request.

Q.7. Did the British government assist Your Majesty, particularly after the Egyptian troops' attack on some of the Aden Protectorate's territories?

A.7. In the aftermath of the coup d'état and the establishment of my counterforce, the British sent a fact-finding mission. I took that mission inside the Yemeni territories and showed them all the territories that were under my control, all the way to the suburbs of Sanaa itself. Later on, when Nasser used the napalm bombs and other chemical weapons against my fellow Yemenis, the British government assisted by transferring a number of those victims to Switzerland for medical treatment. Undoubtedly, Saudi Arabia had paid all the expenses. In addition, Iran provided me with some arms which were paid for by Saudi Arabia, and King Hussein of Jordan sent me a training mission as well as some weapons that were also paid for by Saudi Arabia.

Q.8. How many Egyptians, according to Your Majesty's estimate, were killed in the Yemen War?

A.8. I don't know exactly how many were killed from the Egyptian side, but the Egyptian troops in Yemen reached at one point 100,000 men fully equipped. However, from the Yemeni side, 40,000 Yemenis, civilians and fighters were killed. This high number of casualties happened because the Egyptians had conducted air attacks against the markets (*suqs*) such as the *suqs* of Rabu and Khamis (the markets of Wednesday and Thursday) where Yemenis gathered in high numbers. Those air attacks did not differentiate between civilians and combatants, armed or unarmed citizens. For example, there is an area called al-Murawah. The Egyptians concentrated on its markets and bombarded it several times, killing many, many innocent people.

Q.9. What is Your Majesty's view of the role of Nasser in Yemen in particular, and his role in the Arab world in general?

A.9. Nasser and his men were the real rulers of Yemen after the 1962 coup d'état. At one point, the whole Yemeni government was imprisoned in Cairo. Nasser was trying to dominate the whole Arab world and its nations. He disliked the late King Faisal and considered him his bitter enemy. In early 1960, King Faisal (then Crown Prince Faisal) and I attended one of Nasser's speeches to the Egyptian National Assembly (*Majlis al-Shaib*). After the speech, King Faisal and I came down to congratulate Nasser on the speech and leave the assembly. Nasser hugged King Faisal first and while he was hugging me, he whispered in my ear saying, "Don't think that I hugged Faisal because I like him, on the contrary, I hate him and would love to break his neck." Yes, to this extent Nasser was a disgraceful person. He wanted to control the Arab world, and his policies in Yemen had multi-robes. This policy led him, at once, to realize and discover that all robes were cut-off and he had no one to deal with. On the contrary, King Faisal had one straight-forward policy and never tried to change his policy or follow a multi-policy approach.

Q.10. What does Your Majesty think of the role of the Arab League and the United Nations at that time?

A.10. They both were on a "vacation." Yes, I repeat, they were on a vacation. Even the United Nations' observation mission which came in the aftermath of the so-called "disengagement agreement" [laughing] was inactive and useless.

Q.11. What is Your Majesty's view of the United States' position *vis-à-vis* the coup d'état against you?

A.11. The United States was in full agreement with the coup d'état against me and did not take any action in the beginning. In fact, I wrote a personal letter to President Kennedy, but he did not answer me at all. I also wrote a letter to President de Gaulle of France, who answered me but was not able to help me. However, contrary to President Kennedy, President de Gaulle did not recognize the republican regime.

Q.12. How does Your Majesty explain the Soviet position *vis-à-vis* the coup d'état?

A.12. There is not any doubt that the Soviets knew about the coup d'état in advance due to their friendship with Nasser. They even recognized the new regime during its early hours despite the fact that I was the one who brought them to Yemen. Nevertheless, during the second year of the Civil War, two representatives from the Red Cross came to visit the fighting areas and investigate the Egyptians' use of napalm bombs. During my meeting with them, one of them handed me, from under the table, a piece of paper. This action surprised me, but when I read the paper later on, I found that he wanted to meet me alone. I indeed met with him alone (he was a Swiss). He told me that the Soviets would like to start negotiating with me. I answered him that I was ready to do so if I received a Soviet representative who would ask me officially to negotiate with them. However, nothing happened after that, and I did not receive any Soviet representative or negotiate anything with them.

Q.13. It was said that the Soviets and the Syrians had participated in supporting the republicans after the withdrawal of the Egyptian troops from Yemen in late 1967. What is the truth of this?

A.13. Yes, it is true that the Soviets had participated in the military operations against me and my followers after Nasser's withdrawal from Yemen. In fact, once we shot down a MiG fighter in the area of Kholan and found a dead Soviet pilot inside it. The Syrians, however, did not militarily support the republicans. There were, however, Algerian pilots and combat troops helping the republicans. This Algerian military support resulted from the fact that then Algerian President Ben Bella was a very close friend of Nasser's. I personally, however, did not see those Algerian troops. My followers saw them and reported to me.

Q.14. How did the Civil War end?

A.14. After the Egyptian withdrawal from Yemen, the war continued between the Yemenis themselves, with the exception of a few battles involving Soviet and Algerian combatants, as I have just mentioned. Yemenis were killing each other, a matter which led me to the sole conviction that this kind of war was not in any way beneficial to Yemen itself and her nation. Therefore, I decided to give my followers the freedom to decide their own fate, as well as that of Yemen as a whole. This action on my part led automatically to the Yemeni republican-royalist negotiations supported by Saudi Arabia, which resulted in the solution of the Yemen issue by 1970. I personally did not reject the principle of self-determination by the Yemeni people. In the meantime, I received offers and guarantees from Sheik Abdallah ibn al-Ahmer and from Qadi al-Iryani and others that they were ready to bring out safely the remaining members of the royal family in Yemen. This, in fact, happened and no one was hurt.

Q.15. What is Your Majesty's view of the ongoing issue of unity between North and South Yemen?

A.15. The unity between the two nations existed a long time ago. During my father's time and before that, the two nations were united. However, the unity between the regimes of Ali Abdallah Saleh and Mohammad Ali Nasser is doubtful and I don't think it will materialize in the near future. Nevertheless, if dramatic events happen in the next five-to-ten-year period, one might see that unity take place.

The interview ended at this point and His Majesty promised to write me a "historical document" condemning Nasser's intervention in Yemen and admitting that the Saudi assistance was in accordance with his own request along with other members of the Hamid al-Din family. This document is aimed at clarifying their distorted information about the Saudi role in the Yemen war. At the same time, it is aimed at rejecting and denying many of the pro-Egyptian Yemeni, as well as Egyptian, writers who labelled Saudi Arabia as an aggressive government which had intervened in Yemen in order to wipe out its revolution.

Appendix 3

AGREEMENT BETWEEN
THE UNITED STATES OF AMERICA
AND THE KINGDOM OF THE YEMEN

Signed at Sana'a May 4, 1946

Effective May 4, 1946

The Chief, Special United States Diplomatic Mission to the Kingdom of the Yemen, to the Yemen Deputy Minister of Foreign Affairs

SPECIAL U. S. DIPLOMATIC MISSION
TO THE KINGDOM OF THE YEMEN

SANA'A, *May 4, 1946*

EXCELLENCY:

I have the honor to make the following statement of my Government's understanding of the agreement reached through conversations held at Sana'a April 14 to May 4 by representatives of the Government of the United States of America and the Government of the Kingdom of the Yemen with reference to diplomatic and consular representation, juridical protection, commerce and navigation as hereafter defined. These two Governments, having in mind the letter dated March 4, 1946,[1] from the President of the United States of America to the Imam Yehva Bin Mohamed Hamid-ud-din, King of the Yemen, by which the United States of America recognized the complete and absolute independence of the Kingdom of the Yemen, and desiring to strengthen the friendly relations happily existing between the two countries, and to respect the rights of this independence recognized by the above-mentioned letter as the basis for all their relations and to maintain the most-favored-nation principle in its unconditional and unlimited form as the basis of their commercial relations, agree to the following provisions:

ARTICLE I

The United States of America and the Kingdom of the Yemen will exchange diplomatic representatives and consular officers at a date which shall be fixed by mutual agreement between the two Governments.

ARTICLE II

The diplomatic representatives of each Party accredited to the Government of the other Party shall enjoy in the territories of such other Party the rights, privileges, exemptions and immunities accorded under generally recognized principles of international law. The consular officers of each Party who are assigned to the Government of the other Party, and are duly provided with exequaturs, shall be permitted to reside in the territories of such other Party at the places where consular officers are permitted by the applicable laws to reside; they shall enjoy the honorary privileges and

---

[1] [Not printed.]

the immunities accorded to officers of their rank by general international usage; and they shall not, in any event, be treated in a manner less favorable than similar officers of any third country.

ARTICLE III

Subjects of His Majesty the King of the Yemen in the United States of America and nationals of the United States of America in the Kingdom of the Yemen shall be received and treated in accordance with the requirements and practices of generally recognized international law. In respect of their persons, possessions and rights, such subjects or nationals shall enjoy the fullest protection of the laws and authorities of the country, and shall not be treated in any manner less favorable than the nationals of any third country. Subjects of His Majesty in the United States of America and nationals of the United States of America in the Kingdom of the Yemen shall be subject to the local laws and regulations, and shall enjoy the rights and privileges accorded in this third Article.

ARTICLE IV

In all matters relating to customs duties and charges of any kind imposed on or in connection with importation or exportation or otherwise affecting commerce and navigation, to the method of levying such duties and charges, to all rules and formalities in connection with importation or exportation, and to transit, warehousing and other facilities, each Party shall accord unconditional and unrestricted most-favored-nation treatment to articles the growth, produce or manufacture of the other Party, from whatever place arriving, or to articles destined for exportation to the territories of such other Party, by whatever route. Any advantage, favor, privilege or immunity with respect to any duty, charge or regulation affecting commerce or navigation now or hereafter accorded by the United States of America or by the Kingdom of the Yemen to any third country will be accorded immediately and unconditionally to the commerce and navigation of the Kingdom of the Yemen and of the United States of America, respectively. The advantages relating to customs duties now or hereafter accorded by the United States of America to the Republic of Cuba shall be excepted from the provisions of this agreement.

ARTICLE V

There shall be excepted from the provisions of Article IV of this Agreement advantages now or hereafter accorded: by virtue of a customs union of which either Party may become a member; to adjacent countries in order to facilitate frontier traffic; and by the United States of America or its territories or possessions to one another or to the Panama Canal Zone. The last clause shall continue to apply in respect of any advantages now or hereafter accorded by the United States of America or its territories or possessions to one another irrespective of any change in the political status of any such territories or possessions. Nothing in this Agreement shall prevent the adoption or enforcement by either Party within the area of its jurisdiction: of measures relating to the importation or exportation of gold or silver or the traffic in arms, ammunition, and implements of war, and, in exceptional circumstances, all other military supplies; of measures necessary in pursuance of obligations for the maintenance of international peace and security or necessary for the protection of the essential interests of such Party in time of national emergency; or of statutes in relation to immigration and travel. Subject to the requirement that, under like circumstances and conditions, there shall be no arbitrary discrimination by either Party against the subjects, nationals, commerce or navigation of the other Party in favor of the subjects, nationals commerce or navigation of any third country, the provisions of this Agreement shall not extend to prohibitions or restrictions: imposed on moral or humanitarian grounds; designed to protect human, animal, or plant life or health; relating to prison-made goods; or relating to the enforcement of police or revenue law.

ARTICLE VI

The provisions of this Agreement shall apply to all territory under the sovereignty or authority of either of the parties, except the Panama Canal Zone.

ARTICLE VII

This Agreement shall continue in force until superseded by a more comprehensive commercial agreement, or until thirty days from the date of a written notice of termination given by either party to the other Party, whichever is the earlier. Moreover, either Party may terminate Articles I, II, III, or IV on thirty days written notice.

If the above provisions are acceptable to the Government of the Kingdom of the Yemen this note and the reply signifying assent thereto shall, if agreeable to that Government, be regarded as constituting an agreement between the two Governments which shall become effective on the date of such acceptance.

Accept, Excellency, the assurances of my highest consideration.

WILLIAM A. EDDY
*Chief, Special U. S. Diplomatic Mission
to the Kingdom of the Yemen*

AL QADI ABDUL KARIM MUTAHHAR
*Deputy Minister of Foreign Affairs
Kingdom of the Yemen*

Translation

THE ISLAMIC GOVERNMENT
ORDAINED BY ALLAH

SANA'A
May 4, 1946
Jamada-al-Thaniya, 3, 1365

His Excellency
Mr. WILLIAM ALFRED EDDY
Chief, U. S. Special Mission
to the Kingdom of The Yemen.

I have the honor to acknowledge receipt of Your Excellency's letter dated May 4, 1946, corresponding to Jamada-al-Thaniya, 3, 1365, the text of which is as follows:–

I have the honor to make the following statement of my Government's understanding of the agreement reached through conversations held at Sana'a April 14 to May 4 by representatives of the Government of the United States of America and the Government of the Kingdom of the Yemen with reference to diplomatic and consular representation, juridical protection, commerce and navigation as hereafter defined. These two Governments, having in mind the letter dated March 4, 1946, from the President of the United States of America to the Imam Yehya Bin Mohamed Hamid-ud-din, King of the Yemen, by which the United States of America recognized the complete and absolute independence of the Kingdom of the Yemen, and desiring to strengthen the friendly relations happily existing between the two countries, and to respect the rights of this independence recognized by the above-mentioned letter as the basis for all their relations and to maintain the most-favored-nation principle in its unconditional and unlimited form as the basis of their commercial relations, agree to the following provisions:

ARTICLE I

The United States of America and the Kingdom of the Yemen will exchange diplomatic representatives and consular officers at a date which shall be fixed by mutual agreement between the two Governments.

ARTICLE II

The diplomatic representatives of each Party accredited to the Government of the other Party shall enjoy in the territories of such other Party the rights, privileges, exemptions and immunities accorded under generally recognized principles of international law. The consular officers of each Party who are assigned to the Government of the other Party, and are duly provided with exequaturs, shall be permitted to reside in the territories of such other Party at the places where consular officers are permitted by the applicable laws to reside; they shall enjoy the honorary privileges and the immunities accorded to officers of their rank by general international usage; and they shall not, in any event, be treated in a manner less favorable than similar officers of any third country.

ARTICLE III

Subjects of His Majesty the King of the Yemen in the United States of America and nationals of the United States of America in the Kingdom of the Yemen shall be received and treated in accordance with the requirements and practices of generally recognized international law. In respect of their persons, possessions and rights, such subjects or nationals shall enjoy the fullest protection of the laws and authorities of the country, and shall not be treated in any manner less favorable than the nationals of any third country. Subjects of His Majesty in the United States of America and nationals of the United States of America in the Kingdom of the Yemen shall be subject to the local laws and regulations, and shall enjoy the rights and privileges accorded in this third Article.

ARTICLE IV

In all matters relating to customs duties and charges of any kind imposed on or in connection with importation or exportation or otherwise affecting commerce and navigation, to the method of levying such duties and charges, to all rules and formalities in connection with importation or exportation, and to transit, warehousing and other facilities, each Party shall accord unconditional and unrestricted most-favored-nation treatment to articles the growth, produce or manufacture of the other Party, from whatever place arriving, or to articles destined for exportation to the territories of such other Party, by whatever route. Any advantage, favor, privilege or immunity with respect to any duty, charge or regulation affecting commerce or navigation now or hereafter accorded by the United States of America or by the Kingdom of the Yemen to any third country will be accorded immediately and unconditionally to the commerce and navigation of the Kingdom of the Yemen and of the United States of America, respectively. The advantages relating to customs duties now or hereafter accorded by the United States of America to the Republic of Cuba shall be excepted from the provisions of this agreement.

ARTICLE V

There shall be excepted from the provisions of Article IV of this Agreement advantages now or hereafter accorded; by virtue of a customs union of which either Party may become a member; to adjacent countries in order to facilitate frontier traffic; and by the United States of America or its territories or possessions to one another or to the Panama Canal Zone.

The last clause shall continue to apply in respect of any advantages now or hereafter accorded by the United States of America or its territories or possessions to one another irrespective of any change in the political status of any such territories or possessions. Nothing in this Agreement shall prevent the adoption or enforcement by either Party within the area of its jurisdiction; of measures relating to the importation or exportation of gold or silver or the traffic in arms, ammunition, and implements of war, and, in exceptional circumstances, all other military supplies; of measures necessary in pursuance of obligations for the maintenance or international peace and security or necessary for the protection of the essential interests of such Party in time of national emergency; or of statutes in relation to immigration and travel. Subject to the requirement that, under like circumstances and conditions, there shall be no arbitrary discrimination by either Party against the subjects, nationals, commerce or navigation of the other Party in favor of the subjects, nationals commerce or navigation of any third country, the provisions of this Agreement shall not extend to prohibitions or restrictions: imposed on moral or humanitarian grounds; designed to protect human, animal, or plant life or health; relating to prison-made goods; or relating to the enforcement of police or revenue law.

ARTICLE VI

The provisions of this Agreement shall apply to all territory under the sovereignty or authority of either of the parties, except the Panama Canal Zone.

ARTICLE VII

This Agreement shall continue in force until superseded by a more comprehensive commercial agreement, or until thirty days from the date of a written notice of termination given by either Party to the other Party, whichever is the earlier. Moreover, either Party may terminate Articles I, II, III, or IV on thirty days written notice.

On behalf of the Government of the Yemen, I declare my government's adherence to the provisions stated in this Agreement which is considered effective on the date of signature.

ABDUL KARIM MUTAHHAR
Deputy Foreign Minister

Appendix 4

INTERVIEW WITH HIS EXCELLENCY MAHMOUD RIAD (FORMER EGYPTIAN FOREIGN MINISTER AND SECRETARY-GENERAL OF THE ARAB LEAGUE)

METHODOLOGY: Questions were prepared in advance by the author and written down in Arabic. At the interview, these written questions were submitted to the interviewee, who responded orally in Arabic. The interviewee was permitted to answer uninterrupted, for as long as he deemed it necessary to respond to the question. The author took notes on his answers; no taping of answers was done. After the interview, the author translated his notes on the interviewee's responses into English. The interviewee was not asked to approve the translation.

Cairo, Egypt

Sunday, November 11, 1984

Q.1. Until 1958, Saudi-Egyptian relations were friendly, fruitful and mutually coordinated. Many authors have written that the union between Syria and Egypt was the major factor behind the deterioration of that relation. What is Your Excellency's view?

A.1. Before I answer your question, I would like to mention a number of basic points. The political history of the Arab world is short. This is due to the fact that it was under the control and influence of the colonizing powers. This led to the absence of what is known today in the West as the "political system," i.e., the system that defines, directs and controls a state's policies and strategies. Because of this absence, the political system in our world became completely dependent on the person himself as a ruler, his attitudes and his mood. This ruler, as an

130

ordinary person, is controlled by his ambitions, his wishes and his needs, which in turn are determined by the environment around him. I came to this conclusion after serving in a number of important political posts after the 1952 revolution. Before the revolution, I was in charge of the Palestinian question, which is in my view the main issue for the Arab world. Additionally, in 1954 I was in charge of making and implementing the policies of the Arab world at the Ministry of Foreign Affairs.

With regard to Saudi-Egyptian relations, I would say it was successful, coordinated and characterized by a mutual trust so complete that in 1954 King Saud mediated between Nasser and Mohammed Naguib. This is an extraordinary act because the issue dividing the two was internal and therefore only concerned Egypt.

The year 1955 brought with it the idea of the "Baghdad Pact." Prime ministers of Arab nations met to discuss the idea, and I personally visited a number of Arab capitals in preparation for the meeting. After fifteen sessions, there was total agreement among the conferees to reject the idea. Thereafter, President Nasser declared the need for joint Arab military action, and Saudi Arabia responded positively to the call.

Nasser's declaration was followed by the Tripartite Pact between Egypt, Saudi Arabia and Syria in 1955. Egypt focused on security matters, but Khalid al-Azm, then prime minister of Syria, played an important role in destroying the agreement. Unlike the other leaders, he wanted to join the economies of the three concerned nations in addition to forming a union among them.

In 1956, the well-known Jeddah Military Pact was signed between Egypt, Saudi Arabia and Yemen. Again, it was a security-oriented pact. Here I would like to say that Egypt never attempted to achieve total and complete unity among Arab nations. Egypt was only concerned with security arrangements.

In 1957, Saudi-Egyptian differences began to surface as a result of the general political situation in the Arab world, particularly in Jordan, where the Baathis were attempting to control Jordan as well as Arab politics. In addition, that same year President Shukri al-Kuatli of Syria paid a visit to Egypt, and from there to Saudi Arabia, where he told King Saud that President Nasser was planning to assassinate him, i.e., King Saud. Thereafter, the story of the Egyptian servant who was arrested by the Saudi authorities and accused of planning to plant a bomb in the king's bedroom was circulated. Here I would like to mention that it was the American C.I.A. that was behind the story and the entire plan. The reason is simple. The United States felt that the Saudi-Egyptian closeness worked against its interest in the area. Moreover, there is another reality. That is that the United States was always keen and eager to isolate Egypt from the Arab world, something it was not able to do until 1979 at Camp David. These developments and factors frightened King Saud and changed the course of Saudi policy toward Egypt. This was clearly seen when His Majesty began cooperating with some elements in Syria in 1958 to bring down the Egyptian and Syrian union. The story of the $2 million that was sent by King Saud to those Syrian elements is true. In fact, when King Saud came to Egypt in 1964, he told President Nasser that the amount he sent was $7 million not $2 million and this in turn means that the Syrians did not disclose the full amount and put $5 million into their pockets.

In connection with the union between Egypt and Syria, it was forced on Egypt by the Syrian officers who came to Cairo and met with President Nasser. They themselves asked him to unite the two countries and told him that if the union did not take place a civil war would erupt in Syria among its political parties and sects. President Nasser then had no choice but to accept and accede to their wishes. In fact, Egypt proposed a partial union presented in the form of a five-year plan, but the Syrians insisted on a complete and immediate union. I, myself, was surprised by the announcement and did not know about it until it was announced, despite the fact that I was Egypt's ambassador to Syria at that time. Here, too, one finds that a third hand was behind that event as well, as in the case of the deterioration in Saudi-Egyptian relations. Yemen then joined the federation as well, despite Egypt's initial rejection of the Imam's proposal. Because of Imam Ahmed's insistence, Nasser ultimately agreed to admit Yemen to the union and Yemen became the third member of the federation.

In 1962, the Yemen revolution took place. At that time, Egypt was in a state of shock and frustration as a result of the deterioration of the federation with Syria. From here on you can refer to Ahmed Hamroush's book entitled, *The Story of the July 23 Revolution: Abd al-Nasser and the Arabs*. In it, Hamroush discusses how the Egyptian intervention in Yemen started. He explains that the action started with only two airplanes and about three hundred Egyptian soldiers.

Q.2. Your Excellency has been assigned to a number of high-ranking posts in Egypt, particularly during the critical times in Saudi-Egyptian relations and after the 1962 coup d'état in Yemen, which resulted both in Egyptian military intervention there and in the Saudi moral and financial support to Imam Muhammad al-Badr and his followers. What is your Excellency's opinion about that period?

A.2. Yes, the Yemen war contributed to the deterioration in the Saudi-Egyptian relations. But one thing has to be taken into consideration and that is that the primary reason for Egypt's military intervention in Yemen was to take that country out of the Middle Ages—and not only out of those ages because during that period the Arabs were a civilized nation—but also out of the Dark Ages which Yemeni society was engulfed in. We also must realize that if news of the Imam's death had not reached us, Egypt would not have intervened in Yemen because al-Badr was an open-minded Imam and wanted to bring about a real change in Yemen. Undoubtedly, the Yemen war spoiled the Egyptian army and contributed to the weakening of its morale. However, we must not forget that the same intervention helped South Yemen to get its independence from the British. As you know, all the anti-British South Yemeni groups were headquartered in and operating from Cairo and were receiving Egypt's financial and military support.

Q.3. The late President Anwar al-Sadat played an important role in the Yemen war, and may have also contributed to Egypt's involvement in that war. This has been mentioned by President Nasser himself and Mr. Hassan Sabri al-Kholi.[1] Would your Excellency comment on this?

A.3. Yes. President Nasser relied totally on Anwar al-Sadat *vis-à-vis* the Yemen question. But al-Sadat himself relied on Abd Al-Rahman al-Baidani and his analysis of the situation in Yemen.[2] Because al-Sadat did not like to read, al-Baidani was able to control his mind. Al-Sadat was entirely dependent on al-Baidani's view, and he himself told Ahmed al-Huwwaidi of his plans with al-Baidani as regards Yemen, plans which al-Baidani had formulated. Nevertheless, I repeat that the Egyptian intervention in Yemen moved it, in a brief period of time, from the Dark Ages into the 20th century. Those who saw Yemen in 1962 and then saw it again in 1974 can see the difference between the two periods.

Q.4. A number of agreements were signed between Egypt and Saudi Arabia to solve the Yemen dilemma. A number of peace-loving nations, Arab and non-Arab, invested huge efforts toward the same end. Those efforts were doomed to failure because the signed agreements were not respected. What were the reasons?

A.4. The Yemenis themselves are the principal reason for the failure of those agreements and efforts. They took advantage of the situation by accepting financial support from both Egypt and Saudi Arabia. Therefore, the end of the war and the resolution of the problem were not in the interest of those opportunistic Yemenis. As you and I know, many of those same Yemenis are now millionaires and own businesses in the Arabian Gulf states. For example, Ahmed Farid al-Sarimah, who now owns a big land shipping company in the Gulf, was a leader of a mercenary group during the Yemen war and he benefited financially from it. Yes, it was the Yemenis themselves who were against every agreement and they who prolonged the war in order to satisfy their own greed.

Q.5. It has been said that the Soviet Union played a major role in convincing President Nasser not to respect and abide by the provisions of some of the treaties and agreements he signed with Saudi Arabia. It has also been said that when Nasser signed the 1965 Jeddah Agreement with King Faisal, he was forced to do so because he had asked the Soviets for $20 million worth of weapons to support his war operation in Yemen, but the Soviets hesitated to agree. It has been further said that, after his signing of the Jeddah Agreement, Nasser again bargained with the Russians who then immediately agreed to his demands because they wanted him to stay in Yemen. What is Your Excellency's opinion and information about this?

A.5. It is a fact that each country looks after its own interests, and no one can argue this point. The Russians came to Egypt as a result of American mistakes. In spite of that, they (the Russians) did not play that major a role in Egypt and in the determination of Egypt's foreign policies. During the Yemen crisis, the Russians did not offer any opinions and did not bargain with us. Their main goal was to find a foothold in Yemen. This therefore made them more willing to supply Egypt's needs in Yemen without condition. Between 1954 and 1965, Nasser was famous and at the height of his popularity inside as well as outside the Arab world, and the Russians would not have hesitated to respond to his demands. In my view, Nasser could be compared to Mohammed Ali Pasha because of his strength and determination to turn Egypt into a real regional power. Since the era of Khrushchev, when in the 1950s he tried to force some conditions on Egypt, Nasser's response had been strong and powerful. He made it clear to the Soviets and to other world powers that Egypt could not and would not accept any conditions.[3] Perhaps this stance is the main reason behind the deterioration of relations between Egypt and the United States. The Americans did not understand Nasser, whereas the Russians did. They were therefore able to enter Egypt and to give him what he needed.

Q.6. After the 1968 withdrawal of the Egyptian military forces from Yemen, it was reported that the Soviets militarily supported the republicans and that this support included having Russian pilots participate in the military operations. What does Your Excellency know about this?

A.6. Yes, this is true, but Egypt was not involved at all. The Arab-Israeli War of 1967 and its outcome was a disaster and great shock for us. We started to rebuild ourselves and our army did not want to be involved in any outside operations. The Soviets, as I mentioned earlier, as any other country, have their own political interests and try to promote them.

Q.7. Many Western writers said that one of President Nasser's goals in intervening in Yemen was to gain control of the Arabian Peninsula and the oil resources in the Gulf. Is this true?

A.7. No, this is not true. Our involvement in Yemen was strictly to protect the revolution. It started small as I said before. With regard to the Arabian Peninsula and the oil fields, everyone knows that at the time Egypt was the richest Arab country. We were financially supporting Libya during the Idrisi reign by donating two million Egyptian pounds per year. We were also financially supporting all liberation fronts in the Arab world and Africa. We did not need money from the oil fields.

Q.8. The Arab League, which Your Excellency has served as secretary-general, conducted some efforts and played a noneffective role in attempting to solve the Yemen problem. What are the reasons behind its failure?

A.8. International as well as Arab organizations are always victims of international and regional disputes. They try to carry out their peaceful roles. However, they always face a number of obstacles. This is exactly what happened to the Arab League throughout the Yemen crisis. Also we have to take into consideration two major elements: (1) The personality of the secretary-general himself and his ability to use his powers and the facilities that are rendered to him. (2) The role of the concerned parties, who really have control over the direction of events and political matters. From this we may come to the conclusion that the role of the Arab League in the Yemen problem was not decisive and fruitful because the right person was not available. In the meantime, Egypt and Saudi Arabia themselves were not helpful to the League and its efforts. Here we must recognize a fact and that is that Saudi Arabia and Egypt are the two Arab countries with the most political weight in the Arab world. This is what political events have proved and still prove day after day.

Q.9. The United Nations attempted to conduct and play a constructive role in resolving the Yemen question, especially after the 1964 disengagement agreement was signed by Saudi Arabia and Egypt with the help of the United States. What is Your Excellency's opinion about the U.N. role?

A.9. I regret that international and regional organizations are always victims. As long as the role of the United Nations in the Yemen crisis was not more than as an observer to implement the provisions of the disengagement agreement, the political situation and power usually impose themselves and dictate their rules on the situation as a whole.

That is what happened in Yemen. Therefore, the international organization cannot do anything more than be an observer.

Q.10. What is Your Excellency's view of the current situation in the Arab world, particularly since you left your political post in 1979?

A.10. The Palestinian question is the core and center of Arab politics. When I found in 1979 that there were those who were trying to make it a secondary issue, I preferred to resign my post as secretary-general of the Arab League. Presently, I am trying to write my memoirs and publish them. *Al-Sharq al-Awsat* newspaper published some of those memoirs in a number of articles. President al-Sadat wrote and published his book, *In Search of Identity*; Mohammed Haikal also published a number of books. It is going to be the truth, and nothing but the truth, as I saw it and lived in it.

Notes

[1] Dr. Hassen Sabri Al-Kholi was President Nasser's personal representative in 1964. A veteran of the 1948 Arab-Israeli war, Dr. Al-Kholi was an expert on the Palestinian issue, having written his dissertation on the Palestinian question in addition to publishing a number of books on the subject. As a result of his expertise, Dr. Al-Kholi was appointed head of the Egyptian delegation to the Joint Truce Committee in Palestine. With regard to Yemen, Dr. Al-Kholi was second only to Sadat for his role in formulating Egypt's stance in the Yemeni War. As such, he participated in most of the Yemeni peace negotiations. In 1974, Dr. Al-Kholi was appointed adviser and personal representative of the late President Anwar al-Sadat.

[2] Dr. Abd al-Rahman al-Baidani is a Yemeni citizen who received his undergraduate degree in Islamic Law from Cairo University. He received his Ph.D. in Economics from Bonn University in West Germany. He is married to Jihan al-Sadat's sister. Dr. al-Baidani became vice-chairman of the Revolutionary Council in the Yemen Arab Republic. He was also appointed the minister of economic and foreign affairs in Yemen. In addition, he founded the Yemeni Bank for Construction and Development.

[3] His Excellency was referring to President Nasser's 1958 speech in Damascus.

BIBLIOGRAPHY

Arabic Books

Aql, Muhammad Sadiq and Hiyam Abu Afiyah. *Adwa ala Thawrat al-Yaman* [Lights on the Yemen Revolution]. Cairo: Dar al-Qawmiyah lil-Tibaah wal-Nashr, n.d.

Assah, Ahmed. *Muajizatun fauq al-Rimal* [A Miracle on the Sands], 2nd ed. Beirut: al-Matabi al-Ahliyah al-Lubnaniyah, 1966.

Boyidani, Abd al-Rahman al-. *Azmat al-Umah al-Arabiyah wa Thawrat al-Yaman* [The Crisis of the Arab Nation and the Yemeni Revolution]. Cairo: Matabi al-Maktab al-Misri al-Hadith, 1984.

Butrus Ghali, Butrus. *Al-Jamiyah al-Arabiyah wa Taswiyat al-Munazaat al-Mahalliyah* [The Arab League and the Resolution of Local Disputes]. Cairo: n.p., 1977.

Guzaylan, Lt. General Abdullah al-. *Al-Tarikh al-Sirri lil-Thawrah al-Yamaniyah* [The Secret History of the Yemen Revolution], 2nd ed. Cairo: Maktabat Medbouli, 1979.

Ibn Hazloul, Prince Saud. *Tarikh Muluk al-Saud* [History of the Saudi Kings], 1st ed. Riyadh: Riyadh Press, 1960.

Ibn Misfir, Abdullah ibn Ali. *Akhbar Asir* [News of Asir]. Damascus: al-Maktab al-Islami, 1978.

Mahjub, Muhammad Ahmed. *Al-Dimuqratiyah fil-Mizan* [Democracy in the Balance]. Beirut: Dar Maktabat al-Hayat, 1962.

Narsis, Adnan. *Al-Yaman wa Hadarat al-Arab* [Yemen and Arab Civilization]. Beirut: Dar Maktabat al-Hayat, 1962.

Said, Amin. *Tarikh al-Dawlah al-Saudiyah* [History of the Saudi Dynasty], Vol. 2. Beirut: Dar al-Katib al-Arabi, 1964.

Salamah, Ghassan. *Al-Siyasah al-Kharijyah al-Saudiyah mundhu Am 1945* [Saudi Foreign Policy Since 1945]. Beirut: Muassasat Dar al-Rihani lil-Tibaah wal-Nashr, 1980.

Salim, Sayyid Mustafa. *Takwin al-Yaman al-Hadith: al-Yaman wal-Imam Yahya (1904–1948)* [Structure of Modern Yemen: Yemen and Imam Yahya (1904–1948)]. 3rd ed. Cairo: Maktabat Medbouli, 1984.

Shurayqi, Ibrahim al-. *Al-Sira al-Dami fil-Yaman* [The Bloody Conflict in Yemen], 1st ed. n.p., August 1964.

Yemeni Center for Research and Studies, Sanaa. *Thawrat 26 Sibtambir: Dirasat wa Shahadat lil-Tarikh* [The September 26 Revolution: Studies and Evidence for History]. Beirut: Maktabat al-Jamahir, 1981–82; July 15–18, 1983.

English Books

Ajami, Fouad. *The Arab Predicament*. London, New York, New Rochelle, Melbourne, Sydney: Cambridge University Press, 1981.

Armstrong, H. C. *Lord of Arabia: A Biography of Abdul Aziz Ibn Sa'ud*. Beirut: Khayat's College Book Cooperative, n.d.

Badeau, John S. *The American Approach to the Arab World*. New York, Evanston, London: Harper & Row, 1968.

Bidwell, Robin. *The Two Yemens*. Boulder, CO: Westview Press, 1983.

Copeland, Miles. *The Game of Nations*. New York: College Notes and Texts, 1969.

Cordesman, Anthony H. *The Gulf and the Search for Strategic Stability: Saudi Arabia, the Military Balance in the Gulf, and Trends in the Arab-Israeli Military Balance*. Boulder, CO: Westview Press; London: Mansell Publishing, 1984.

Cremeans, Charles D. *The Arabs and the World: Nasser's Arab Nationalist Policy*. New York: Frederick A. Praeger, 1963.

Faroughy, Abbas. *Introducing Yemen*. New York: Orientalia, 1947.

Farsy, Fouad al-. *Saudi Arabia: A Case Study in Development*. London: Stacey International, 1980.

Fisher, Sydney Nettleton. *The Middle East: A History*. New York: Knopf, 1959.

De Gaury, Gerald. *Faisal: King of Saudi Arabia*. London: Arthur Barker, 1966.

Goldman, Marshall I. *Soviet Foreign Aid*. New York, 1967.

Gordon, Murray, ed. *Conflict in the Persian Gulf*. New York: Facts on File, 1981.

Gros, Marill. *Feisal of Arabia: The Ten Years of Reign*. England: EMG'E, SPIX, 1976.

Halliday, Fred. *Arabia Without Sultans*. New York: Vintage Books, 1975.

Hassouna, Hussein A. *The League of Arab States and Regional Disputes: A Study of Middle East Conflicts*. Dobbs Ferry, New York: Oceana; Leiden: A. W. Sijthoff, 1975.

Holden, David, and Richard Johns. *The House of Saud*. New York: Holt, Rinehart and Winston, 1981.

Hudson, Michael C. *Arab Politics: The Search for Legitimacy*. New Haven: Yale University Press, 1977.

Hurewitz, J. C. *Middle East Politics: The Military Dimension*. New York, Washington, London: F. A. Praeger, 1969.

Ingrams, Harold. *The Yemen*. New York: Praeger, 1964.

Kerr, Malcolm H. *The Arab Cold War: Gamal 'Abd al-Nasir and His Rivals, 1958–1970*, 3rd ed. London: Oxford University Press, 1971.

Khalil, Mohammed, ed. *The Arab States and the Arab League*, vol. II. Beirut: Khayats, 1962.

Lacey, Robert. *The Kingdom: Arabia & the House of Sa'ud*. New York: Avon Books, 1981.

Lenczowski, George. *The Middle East in World Affairs*, 4th ed. Ithaca: Cornell University Press, 1980.

Long, David, and Bernard Reich, eds. *The Government and Politics of the Middle East and North Africa.* Boulder, CO: Westview Press, 1980.

McLane, Charles. *Soviet–Middle East Relations.* London, 1973.

McMullen, Christopher J. *Resolution of the Yemen Crisis 1963: A Case Study in Mediation.* Washington, DC: Institute for the Study of Diplomacy, School of Foreign Service, Georgetown University, 1980.

Macro, Eric. *Yemen and the Western World.* New York: Frederick A. Praeger Publishers, 1968.

Mansfield, Peter. *Nasser's Egypt.* Baltimore: Penguin Books, 1965.

National Association of Arab Americans. *Middle East Business Survey.* Washington, DC, 1982.

O'Ballance, Edgar. *The War in Yemen.* London: Faber and Faber, 1971.

O'Brien, William B. *U.S. Military Intervention: Law and Morality.* Beverly Hills: Sage Publications, 1979.

Organization for Economic Cooperation and Development Assistance Committee, *Development Cooperation Efforts, 1982 Review,* cited in Peterson, J. E. *Yemen: The Search for a Modern State.* Baltimore: The Johns Hopkins University Press, 1982.

Peterson, J. E., ed. *The Politics of Middle Eastern Oil.* Washington, DC: Middle East Institute, 1983.

Quandt, William B. *Saudi Arabia in the 1980s: Foreign Policy, Security, and Oil.* Washington, DC: The Brookings Institution, 1981.

Sadat, Anwar al-. *In Search of Identity.* New York: Harper Colophon Books, 1978.

Salah, Said. *Panorama of Saudi Arabia.* Dhahran, Saudi Arabia, and distributed by IOA, 1976, revised and enlarged in 1978.

Schmidt, Dana A. *Yemen: The Unknown War.* New York: Holt, Rinehart and Winston, 1968.

Sharabi, Hisham B. *Nationalism and Revolution in the Arab World.* New York: Van Nostrand Reinhold, 1966.

Shaw, John, and David E. Long. *Saudi Arabian Modernization: The Impact of Change on Stability.* New York: Praeger, for the Georgetown University Center for Strategic and International Studies, Washington Paper No. 89, 1982.

Stookey, Robert. *Yemen: The Politics of the Yemen Arab Republic.* Boulder, CO: Westview Press, 1978.

von Glahn, Gerhard. *Law Among Nations: An Introduction to Public International Law,* 4th ed. New York: Macmillan Publishing Co., Inc., 1981.

Wenner, Manfred W. *Modern Yemen: 1918–1966.* Baltimore: The Johns Hopkins Press, 1967.

Yodfat, Aryeh Y. *The Soviet Union and the Arabian Peninsula.* London: Croom Helm, 1983.

Zabarah, Mohammed Ahmed. *Yemen: Tradition vs. Modernity.* New York: Praeger, 1982.

Periodicals

Al-Ahram, October 1, 1962; November 16, 1962.

Al-Sharq al-Awsat, October 17, 1984.

Arab Report and Record, May 16–31, 1965; August 1–15, 1966; August 16–31, 1967.

BBC. Summary of World Broadcast (SWB), October 1962.

Brown, William R. "The Yemeni Dilemma." *The Middle East Journal*, vol. 17, no. 4 (Autumn 1963).

Campbell, John C. "The Soviet Union in the Middle East." *The Middle East Journal*, vol. 32, no. 1 (Winter 1978).

――――. "The Middle East: A House of Containment Built on Shifting Sands." *Foreign Affairs*, Special Issue on "America and the World," (1981).

――――. "Soviet Strategy in the Middle East." *American-Arab Affairs*, no. 8 (Spring 1984).

Cot, Jean Pierre. "Winning East-West in North-South." *Foreign Policy*, no. 46 (Spring 1982).

Dawisha, A. I. "Intervention in the Yemen: An Analysis of an Analysis of Egyptian Perceptions and Politics." *The Middle East Journal*, vol. 29, no. 1 (Winter 1978).

"The Dilemmas of the U.S. Policy Towards the Gulf." *Institute for Defense Studies and Analyses Journal* (IDSA Journal), vol. 12, no. 1 (July-September 1979).

Dobert, Margarita. "Development of Aid Programs to Yemen." *American-Arab Affairs*, no. 8 (Spring 1984).

The Economist, April 3, 1965.

Foreign Reports Bulletin (FRB), October 10, 12, 1962; November 13, 30, 1962; December 5, 26, 1962.

Ghurab, Wahib Muhammad. "The Second Gulf Summit" (in Arabic). *Al-Majallah*, no. 93 (November 21–22, 1983).

Hart, Jane Smiley. "Basic Chronology for a History of the Yemen." *The Middle East Journal*, vol. 17, nos. 1 and 2 (Winter and Spring 1963).

Heyworth-Durne, J. "The Yemen." *Middle Eastern Affairs*, vol. IX, no. 2 (February 1958).

Hottinger, Arnold. "Arab Communism at Low Ebb." *Problems of Communism*, no. 30 (July-August 1981).

Kelly, J. B. "The Future in Arabia." *International Affairs*, vol. 41 (October 1966).

Khoury, Nabeel A. "The Pragmatic Trend in Inter-Arab Politics." *The Middle East Journal*, vol. 36, no. 3 (Summer 1982).

Koury, Enver M. "The Impact of the Geopolitical Situation of Iraq upon the Gulf Cooperation Council." *Middle East Insight*, vol. 2, no. 5 (1983).

Al-Majallah, May 9–15, 1983; November 21–22, 1983.

Middle East Affairs, vols. 13–14, 1962–63.

Middle East Business Survey. Washington, DC: National Association of Arab-Americans, 1982.

Moss, Robert. "Reaching for Oil: The Soviets Bold Mideast Strategy." *Saturday Review*, vol. 7, no. 8 (April 12, 1980).

The New York Times, June 16, 1963; May 13, 1964; April 10, 1970.

Newsweek, November 26, 1962.

Page, Stephen. "Moscow and the Arabian Peninsula." *American-Arab Affairs*, no. 8 (Spring 1984).

Price, David Lynn. "Moscow and the Persian Gulf." *Problems of Communism*, no. 38 (March-April 1979).

Quandt, William B. "Saudi Arabia Security and Foreign Policy in the 1980's." *Middle East Insight*, vol. 2, no. 2 (1983).

Reich, Bernard. "The Soviet Union and the Middle East." *Social Science and Policy Research*, vol. II, no. 21, December 1980.

Rentz, George. "The Fahd Peace Plan." *Middle East Insight*, vol. 2, no. 2 (1983).

"Revolutionary Gains," *Newsweek*, April 3, 1967.

Scott, Hugh. "The Yemen in 1937–1938." *Journal of the Royal Central Asian Society*, vol. XXVII, part 1 (January 1940).

Serjeant, R. B. "The Two Yemens: Historical Perspectives and Present Attitudes." *Asian Affairs*, vol. 60, no. 1 (February 1973).

Sullivan, Robert R. "Saudi Arabia in International Politics." *Review of Politics*, vol. 32 (1979).

The Times (London). September 28, 1962.

"The Undeclared War," *The New Republic*, no. 149 (August 3, 1963).

United Nations Review (UNR), vol. 10, 1963.

"Yemen: The War and the Haradh Conference." *Review of Politics*, vol. 28, no. 3 (July 1966).

Unpublished Papers and Private Sources

Goseibi, Ghazi Abdul-Rahman al-. "The 1962 Revolution in Yemen and Its Impact on the Foreign Policies of the U.A.R. and Saudi-Arabia." Ph.D. Dissertation, University College, University of London, 1970.

Ross, Lee Ann. "The Yemeni Remittance Agent." Unpublished paper written for the United States Agency for International Development, Yemen Mission, May 1979.

United Nations. Report of the Secretary-General to the Security Council concerning the development relating to Yemen, Document S/5298, April 29, 1963.

The following papers were presented at the "Symposium on Contemporary Yemen," Center for Arab Gulf Studies, University of Exeter, July 15–18, 1983

Al-Abiadh, Ahmed. "Modernization of Government Institutions: 1962–1982."

Al-Kasir, Ahmed. "The Impact of Emigration on the Social Structure in Yemen Arab Republic."

Braun, Ursula. "Prospects for Yemeni Unity."

Douglas, Leigh. "The Free Yemeni Movement: 1935–62."

El Azhary, S. M. "Aspects of North Yemen's Relations with Saudi Arabia."

Meyer, Gunter. "Labor Emigration and International Migration in the Yemen Arab Republic—Illustrated by the Example of Employees in the Urban Building Sector." West Germany: Department of Geography, University of Erlangen-Nurnberg.

Nagy, Sutton. "The Crisis of the Call for Yemeni Unity."

Peterson, J. E. "The Challenge of Political Development in the Two Yemens."

Rajab, A. Taher. "The Development of the Banking Sector in the Yemen Arab Republic."

Saggaf, Y. Abdulaziz. "Fiscal and Budgetary Policies in the YAR."

Sresh, Paul. "Tribal Relations in Upper Yemen," Oxford: St. John's College, March 1983.

Zabarah, A. Mohammed. "The Yemeni Revolution of 1962 Seen as a Social Revolution."

[The above have been published as *Contemporary Yemen: Political and Historical Background,* B. R. Pridham, ed. (London: Croom Helm, 1984).]

Interviews

Interviews conducted with Saudi, Yemeni and Egyptian officials and with scholars expert in the subject matter of this work constituted a crucial primary source of information. Many of these individuals were directly involved in the conflict and in the decisionmaking processes that affected its course and agreed to be interviewed only on the grounds that they would not be directly cited in the dissertation. Some of the more prominent individuals who are referred to in this work include the ex-Imam of Yemen, Muhammad al-Badr, and H.E. Mahmoud Riad, former foreign minister of Egypt. The full texts of the interviews with these individuals are included in the appendices to this study.

INDEX